EZEKIEL'S BONES

Rekindling Your Congregation's
Spiritual Passion

BILL KEMP

DISCIPLESHIP RESOURCES

PO BOX 340003 • NASHVILLE, TN 37203-0003
www.discipleshipresources.org

Cover design by Christa Schoenbrodt.

ISBN 13: 978-0-88177-498-6

Library of Congress Cataloging-in-Publication Data

Kemp, Bill, 1954-
  Ezekiel's bones : rekindling your congregation's spiritual passion /
Bill Kemp.
    p. cm.
  ISBN 978-0-88177-498-6
  I. Christian leadership. I. Title.
  BV652.I.K46 2007
  269—dc22

                                    2007007524

Contents

Preface

Yours may be a church with low spiritual passion if:

- People believe that the best days of this church are in the past.

- No one can remember the last time someone helped someone else become a Christian.

- People mention prayer concerns in worship, but fail to praise God when prayer is answered.

- The church council spends endless hours making plans and setting goals, but the same things happen year after year.

- Less than half of the regular church attendees participate in a Bible study or small group for spiritual growth.

- People worry about fixing the church roof, but not about helping their neighbor to know Jesus.

- Even the minister is bored with worship.

- Not only does the congregational life feel down, the numbers reflect it. Few people attend worship, children do not participate in Sunday school, and the church needs volunteers to run the programs of the church.

- The key church leaders won't gather for extended periods of prayer or model their own spiritual disciplines for others to follow.

- Fun times in fellowship and good things to eat at the church picnic abound, but lack expressions of joy in the Lord.

When young people in love are passionate about each other, you know it. If your congregation is passionate about God, you will know it in the same way.

If you want to rekindle that flame, read on.

CHAPTER ONE

What Is Spiritual Passion and Why Do We Need It?

Just dropped in to see what condition my condition is in.

"Just Dropped In (To See What Condition My
Condition Is In)" by Mickey Newbury.

One of the great bug-a-boos of life is our propensity for getting into a rut. As individuals we fall into comfortable habits and become attached to familiar rituals. It may be the routine of eating the same breakfast every day or preferring a particular style of clothing. Our ruts can also have a more sinister side, supporting our prejudices, restricting our generosity, stifling our creativity, derailing our spiritual experience, and instilling within us a reluctance to implement needed changes. Those recovering from dangerous dependencies, such as drug addiction, know how high the walls of routine can become once validated by our physiology, psychology, or spiritual condition. If we were wise, we would choose our ruts more carefully, for we travel in them a long time.

Congregations, too, fall into ruts. Traditions can become so familiar and comfortable that small changes to the weekly ritual feel like mortal sin. As churches move deeper into their ruts, they become hidden within their neighborhoods. Their programs and worship services lack relevance, creativity, and vitality. The emotional side of the congregation's spiritual experience—its passion—fades. Churches can treat the personal experience of God as an unnecessary interruption to the more important business of the church. The church prays, but lacks any expectation of being acted upon by God. The church praises a holy and awesome God, but sings ho-hum hymns. A church can travel so far within its own little groove that it can no longer see how much its neighbors long to know God. When congregations cease being excited about bringing the good news of Jesus to others, they cease to be exciting.

A congregation can be in this downward path for a long time without being aware that it has walked away from the activity of God. To be a people separated from God is to be a people who have lost their real love.

Jeremiah hears God say, "I remember the devotion of your youth, how as a bride you loved me . . . " (Jeremiah 2:2).

As an individual, are you still passionate about God? What about your congregation and the other church leaders who work with you? Can you feel the heartbeat of your congregation's desire for the Almighty? Many congregations today have sacrificed the joy of a living faith for the security of a predictable religion. Even though this behavior may be done with quality, the church still travels in the rut of spiritual mediocrity. Something has been lost.

God offers Jeremiah this explanation for the state of the congregation, "My people have committed two sins: They have forsaken me, the spring of living water, and have dug their own cisterns, broken cisterns that cannot hold water" (Jeremiah 2:13).

No committee at your church may ever have voted to lower the congregation's expectations of God. A motion may never have reached your council urging you to abandon God or to forsake the task of being faithful witnesses, aggressively engaging the surrounding culture. Yet here you may be, lacking spiritual passion for today's religious race. Loss of zeal for the Lord is not the fruit of one bad choice or the fault of certain people in the congregation. It is, instead, woven into the very culture of the organization and evident in many things we do or fail to do each week.

What It Feels Like

Low spiritual passion is like a governor that limits the speed of a motor, or an illness that limits one's breath or mobility. The church finds itself asthmatic in its praise of God and unable to articulate why one would want to be a Christian. The church finds itself arthritic in its mission and unwilling to implement new programs. Low spiritual passion is similar to the condition known as chronic depression. The congregation has a certain dullness of religious feeling and a bland acceptance of the content of the gospel without an awareness of its relevance. Joy diminishes and there is a reluctance to admit that joy is possible.

For some churches low spiritual passion is a progressively disabling condition. Unless reversed, these churches will fade away until their youth scatter and their buildings sell. The cause of their closure may be attributed to conflict, structural problems, or lack of leadership, but the thing that weakened them was the loss of spiritual passion. I am convinced that many congregations engage in self-destructive behavior, such as nurturing conflict, to keep from facing the reality of their spiritual diseases.

Your congregation may not be this extreme. In a less acute form, lowered spiritual passion keeps the leadership team off message and less confident about the church's mission and outreach. The membership may know that something is wrong, but feels powerless to change things. An outsider visiting the church may find many things they like about the church, but still feel that something is missing.

The spiritually depressed congregation does not need to change its identity or forget its former days. When a doctor treats an individual for clinical depression, the goal of the therapy and prescribed medication is not to alter the person's identity or to change the content of his or her memories. Instead, the treatment returns the brain chemistry back to normal and provides better tools for the individual to understand his or

her experiences and respond to life's changes. In a similar fashion, congregations with low spiritual passion do not need to change everything.
They do, however, need to realize that it is normal to feel good about
faith. Further, they need to practice new behaviors that will shift their
attitudes about prayer, scripture, and the sharing of their faith. The
proof that the depression has lifted comes when they become enthusiastic about sharing who they are as a congregation with those around them
who don't have a church home.

Old Realities Verses New

Besides feeling out of breath, arthritic, and depressed, low spiritual
passion feels old. Our culture glorifies the new and improved, often
making congregations feel as if they are out of the race just because they
were established in the previous century and espouse a faith that is two
millennia old. This book will focus upon eliminating the structures of
spiritual mediocrity that keep us busy doing activities unrelated to our
love of God. Examples of passionate Christianity are found today in
every denomination, in congregations old and new, large and small.
Throughout the ages, saints and congregations have maintained their
spiritual passion by focusing on four things: prayer scripture, witness,
and worship. Spiritual passion relates to the way that a church is in love
with God.

PRAYER

In some churches, prayer feels very old and out of touch. Before
meetings, a perfunctory prayer is said before the "real" business begins.
At worship the congregation mumbles or sits silently, eyes shut, longing
for an "amen" while their pastor stumbles through the same interces-
sions week after week. A few in the congregation pray for the sick in
hopes that thinking of them might make them feel better. In fact, the
whole reality of prayer as a process of inviting our holy God to inter-
vene in specific human situations has been substituted for a definition of
prayer which involves doing little more than thinking good thoughts.
Any concerns for the world beyond are briefly mentioned in politically

non-offensive language. All present, even the pastor, are struggling to resist the urge to yawn. The church has entered into the rut of prayer without expectation.

SCRIPTURE

Much has been done over the last sixty years to put the Bible into contemporary language. Vibrant churches take these new tools and run into the deeper problem of putting the Bible into contemporary people. Yet the hidden attitude of congregations with lowered spiritual passion is that the Bible is inherently old. The laity may exhibit a certain false humility, stating that since they are not trained they cannot hope to understand an ancient text subject to so many differing interpretations. The congregation's leaders may have fallen into the post-modern mindset that questions the existence of absolute truth (all is relative) and doubts that any text, no matter how divinely inspired, can be relevant to a variety of cultures. This line of thinking undercuts not only the congregation's support of foreign mission, but also their willingness to share their faith with their own children. Yet people who come to love God also come to love God's word and see it as a living entity speaking to contemporary culture. They feel joy in fulfilling the command of Deuteronomy, "Impress [God's words] on your children. Talk about them when you sit at home and when you walk along the road, when you lie down and when you get up" (Deuteronomy 6:7).

WITNESS

If there is one place that churches with low spiritual passion feel modern, it is in their attitude about not offending others with their beliefs. When religion becomes a personal and private matter, then it becomes unspeakable. There is a basic law of human nature, both for individuals and for congregations: what we do not speak about is what we do not care about. The very purpose of ritual is to give voice to that which is mysterious, and by speaking it, to give it honor. Congregations that deepen their love for God become more verbal about their faith and more systematic in their outreach and witness. They encourage people to talk about their personal faith in new ways. The challenge of doing this in today's contemporary world propels these laity to deepen their knowledge of scripture and commitment to prayer.

WORSHIP

If anything shouts the word "boring," it is worship services that have lost the flame of passion. Spiritually passionate churches can have services steeped in traditional liturgies, provided that the experience leaves the participants energized to live the Christian gospel with enthusiasm. I sense that the movement of the Holy Spirit today is not towards making all successful churches look alike, but towards a diversity of worship practices where each congregation finds fulfillment in its own way of expressing its love for God.

Moving from old realities and attitudes about prayer, scripture, witness, and worship, will require the breaking of old bad habits. Congregational habits are hard to break.

A Systemic Problem

Congregations, even the smallest, are highly complex social systems. There may be a general agreement among the various volunteers and staff that Old First Church is going through a bit of a spiritual decline, and that there has been a noticeable loss of energy lately. A number of the leaders may even be aware of the current membership trends and be concerned about their failure to attract new people. Sidebar discussions at the church council meetings may even have identified a culprit or two. Some may be convinced that if the preacher could deliver more interesting sermons, or if the hallways could be painted a brighter color, all would be well. Low spiritual passion, however, is usually a system-wide problem. The causes of low spiritual passion lie buried in the congregation's history, and its tentacles reach into every aspect of church life.

Picture a congregation like a mobile hanging over a baby's crib. Touching one object on the mobile will generate vibrations throughout the whole structure. Lifting one of the dangling objects, however, will not cause all of the objects to rise. Brightening the paint in the hallways or switching to a more upbeat contemporary worship style will not energize the whole church. In fact, lifting one thing may cause another thing to go down. In the typical church, every group and committee is interconnected by strings of informal relationships. When specific actions are implemented to raise a congregation's spiritual passion, it is helpful to keep in mind the big picture. Each of the implementation chapters of this book will emphasize attempting small changes across every aspect of the church's life, rather than focusing one major cure-all.

Without exception, a congregation's leadership will express their desire to do what is best for their church and to support all necessary changes. It is human nature, however, to be protective of ones own turf and to perpetuate practices that have become familiar and habitual. Each leader will contribute his or her inertia and resistance to participating in new behaviors. They will question expenditures and greet new ideas with the phrase, "We've never done it that way before."

Elevating the spiritual passion of a congregation requires more than simply passing a motion at the church council or engaging the pastor's interest in the subject. It is not the type of task that can be delegated to a committee, even though beginning with a small group of people committed to pray together about the issue is recommended. In the end, the whole of the church leadership will need to be brought on board. The vision of a more spiritually vibrant church will need to be propagated throughout the congregational system. Not everyone will understand or buy into this vision, but those that do will sacrificially invest their reputations, time, and resources to birth a radically reformed organization. These first adopters in the church are like salt or the leaven of Jesus' parables (Matthew 5:13, 13:33). They may learn new skills, becoming local experts on the subject of how spiritual passion relates to the activities of their own committee or church position. Following their lead, others will evaluate their own behavior and ask themselves, "To what degree do I model a heartfelt love for the Lord?" You may phrase this question in a variety of ways, but its sentiment forms the watchword of an organization that is changing the way it feels about the things of God.

Getting out of the rut called low spiritual passion requires more than a gifted pastor or the church's participation in some new program. It requires the refocusing of the whole congregation's attention upon the problem. The church as a whole must set its sights on becoming reborn (John 3:3-8). Churches would do well to remember the words of Bob Dylan, "that he [who is] not busy being born, is busy dying" ["It's Alright, Ma (I'm Only Bleeding)" by Bob Dylan, 1965.] This counter-cultural motto of the 1960s has become a stark word of prophesy for the low spiritual passion church of the new millennium. No, not every passionless church is teetering on the verge of closure. Nor is every declining church suffering from low spiritual passion. Sustainability requires constant rebirth of a congregation's enthusiasm and passion for God.

This rebirth is often painful. Jesus spoke about his Father pruning the grape vine to make it productive (John 15:2). Systemic change neces-sitates organizational change. Rebirth requires old leadership and old ways of doing things to move aside to cultivate new leaders and leader-ship techniques. Conflict may erupt, people committed to the old familiar culture may abandon their leadership posts, and long-time members may threaten to leave. New members and people who were not given an opportunity to serve, however, always arise to fill these vacant positions.

Congregations that rebound from decline often credit their pastor for turning them around and causing them to grow. This does not mean that dying congregations need to look only for the right pastor. Like all congregational problems, low spiritual passion does not emanate from the pulpit, but is woven into the church's life. Where clergy leadership has initiated the change, it has always been with the help of committed laity who entered into a team relationship with their staff. All real trans-formation in congregations builds upon people first becoming open to the moving of the Spirit in their own lives, and then being willing to become leaders in new and varied ways, stretching these innovators far beyond what they formerly thought possible.

Making Your Church Fly

Imagine your congregation as an airplane and yourself as its pilot. Your congregation may be a big 747 with hundreds of people on board, or a small commuter turbo-prop with fifty cramped seats. No matter how many are flying with you, being a leader in your congregation makes you responsible for the spiritual lives of others. If the church were to close, how many of the people currently worshiping with you will find another place to nurture and support their faith? Worse yet, what if your plane remains on the runway and never takes people to their destination? Planes are meant to fly, and one of the assumptions of this book is that Christ has called your congregation to fly. Jesus revealed a destination for his people when he gave his disciples the parting command that they, in turn, make more disciples (Matthew 28:19). A congregation where people are not committed to faith sharing is unlikely to arrive at that destination. A congregation where the people do not routinely invite others to join them in worship is not flying. A congregation where prayer is rote ritual and the Bible irrelevant is unlikely to get off the ground.

Taking your responsibilities seriously, both as a congregational leader and as pilot, you carefully check your instrument panel. Since you picked this book up, I suspect that the fuel gauge is the first place you are going to look. A church without spiritual passion is like a plane running on empty. An airline may have wonderful flight attendants, cheap fares, serve meals, and have great in-flight movies, but if it lets its planes take off with insufficient fuel, not many people will want to fly it. Not only is the practice dangerous, people headed for the coast generally don't like the idea of having to make a pit stop in St. Louis because somebody didn't think having enough fuel was as important as choosing a great in-flight movie.

Denominational leaders rarely ask congregations to evaluate whether or not they have sufficient spiritual passion to reach the destination of making more disciples. Yearly statistical reports do not measure the critical fuel tanks of prayer, Bible use, witness, and worship. Pastors rarely express concerns about their congregation's lack of enthusiasm when they choose continuing education resources or dialogue about their church work. It is unusual for lay leadership to openly discuss how their congregation's heart-felt love of God, or lack there of, affects their ongoing task of gaining new members. At every level, church leaders put more emphasis upon beautiful buildings, fine choirs, friendly potluck suppers, and well-typed bulletins, even though none of these external things can bring growth and vitality to a church that is no longer passionate about God.

Is spiritual passion a measurable thing, like fuel on a gauge? I say yes, which is why there are three evaluative exercises in this book. People who are searching for a church will remark about how one church feels full of the Spirit and another feels dry. They are speaking about an objective reality that their intuitive instincts have somehow measured. Spiritual passion also contributes to the statistics that measure the growth of a congregation relative to the population of their community. Churches with low spiritual passion never grow, no matter what the population around them is doing, and churches with high spiritual passion can grow even in a community that is experiencing economic hardship and an exodus of young adults (see the example of Grace Lutheran in chapter six). Further, increases in spiritual passion in a church usually result in a dramatic rise in financial contributions (see chapter eight). Yet for some reason, congregations often ignore spiritual passion when assessing their own strengths and weaknesses or when making long range plans.

Constantly worrying about whether or not you have enough fuel to make it to the next stop can lead to leadership burnout. Church workers in an environment that fails to emphasize the power of prayer, the relevance of scripture, or the joy of worship and witness will feel less rewarded when their hard work helps others know these things. Seeing the parents of his or her charges able to go to worship does not reward the nursery worker who secretly thinks that the worship service is dull. The congregant will grow reluctant to contribute to foreign missions, if he or she isn't convinced that others need the same gospel that he or she received through the witness of this congregation. We all will grow weary of doing good, as the Apostle Paul reminds us, if we lose sight of the harvest (Galatians 6:9). Low spiritual passion directly contributes to leadership burnout by devaluing the way we feel about our service to the Lord, and thus lowers the threshold before we feel what we are doing doesn't matter.

The Grassroots-Up Approach

Deeply rooted aspects of an organization's behavior only change from the bottom up. Studying the soil or the context of the congregation's current culture is an important first step. A grassroots approach to raising spiritual passion in a congregation might look like the following:

STEP ONE: NAME THE PROBLEM

Sometimes it helps to get an outside consultant to voice another opinion on the congregation's condition. The evaluative exercises of this book are handouts for use as discussion starters to get people seeing beyond what they have become accustomed to seeing. It is important that the term "spiritual passion" gets placed on the congregational radar screen.

STEP TWO: FORM A PRAYER AND STUDY GROUP

A small group of people sets out to learn together, perhaps reading and sharing together a resource such as this book. They study current reality. They prayerfully seek to understand the purpose God might have for this church. They make a covenant to meet together for an extended period, such as for two hours each Sunday night throughout the season of Lent. They agree to remember each other in their daily prayer time and to pray about the spiritual needs of the congregation.

STEP THREE: BUILD CONGREGATIONAL AWARENESS

Over the course of a month or two, a variety of prayer experiences, small study groups, and worship themes spread awareness about the issue. Unlike the first two steps, this step emphasizes the positive truth that God is willing to rebirth God's church. Encouraging sermons and newly formed study groups fuel a longing among the people for a passionate experience of Christianity. The whole church might join in studying the early chapters of Acts or other passages that show the power of a community that has rediscovered their love of God.

STEP FOUR: RAISE THE BAR

An expectation builds throughout the church for every member to become a part of a small group for their own spiritual formation. People begin to hold each other accountable for personal spiritual disciplines, such as regular times for intercessory prayer, intensive study of the Bible, and sacrificial giving.

STEP FIVE: REQUIRE SPIRITUAL DISCIPLINES

This change challenges church leaders to alter the way their groups, committees, or teams function, so as to incorporate a greater emphasis on prayer and discernment in their decision making process. The church council adopts a list of basic expectations for people in leadership, which may include statements such as, "All committee chairs will be faithful members of a small group for prayer and study" or, "Group leaders will participate in one workshop or read one book related to their area of service each year."

STEP SIX: ENABLE NEW LEADERSHIP

Train new people and bring them onboard to replace those who were reluctant to work at raising spiritual passion or meeting the council's list of basic expectations. A leadership shift takes place that gives positions only to Christians with personal lives marked by passionate spirituality. Every leader sees his or her primary task as raising the congregation's love for God.

STEP SEVEN: IMPLEMENT NEW PROGRAMS AND PROJECTS

The momentum of spiritual change now makes it possible for the church to launch into new activities, such as starting a contemporary worship service or developing an outreach to their unchurched neighbors. Interest increases in learning how to share one's faith. New programs begin to help every participant in the church move towards a more intense love for God and a willingness to share God's love with others.

Self Evaluation

The marks of low spiritual passion are:

✓ A reluctance to witness or share faith with others;

✓ A lack of genuine expectation of prayer to change things;

✓ A loss of interest in studying the Bible or expecting it to have truth that can be applied to daily life;

✓ An inability to show any joy when talking about faith;

✓ A lifeless feel to worship, even though the worship performance may be of excellent quality;

✓ A disconnect between the work of the church's committees and the faith that the church professes, that is, what we believe doesn't affect what we do;

✓ A loss of hope for the future coupled with a reluctance to try new things.

The Need for Objectivity

It is hard to be objective about one's own church. You may have come to faith in this congregation. How can you accept that your church has become spiritually dry? You may be the pastor of a declining congregation. How can you receive a diagnosis that implies that your spiritual leadership has been ineffective? On the other hand, you may be a newcomer to this particular congregation, and its rituals and expectations are still a mystery to you. How can you initiate a process that will help your newfound friends become more spiritually alive? No matter what your position or history with a congregation, bringing about systemic change within a congregation is a difficult task.

The task of bringing about systematic change begins with objective and specific congregational assessment. At the end of this chapter is an exercise for diagnosing your churches condition. It has both an objective and subjective component. It is important not to ignore the objective statistical path of steady decline that is symptomatic of low spiritual passion. While few people drive their cars regularly without checking their fuel gauge, many congregations refuse to give their leadership regular access to the statistics that track their success at attracting and retaining new members. Sometimes a ten-year track of average worship attendance shocks staid church councils into action as they begin to realize a time is coming when no one will use their beloved sanctuary. Church leaders should also regularly have more subjective group discussions about their congregation's strengths and weaknesses. Rather than simply airing grievances, these discussions should prayerfully discern the telltale surface signs of deeper problems and the hidden costs of missed opportunities.

When Jesus began his ministry among the people of Galilee, he faced the challenge of assessing and bringing about change in the very congregations that he himself had grown up and where his family ties were well known. It was frustrating work, having to speak truthfully about the people who were significant to his faith development. His words, "no prophet is accepted in his hometown" (Luke 4:24), ring true with anyone who has ever tried to bring about change in a social system to which they belong. Jesus did, however, speak accurately and critically about his home congregations. He noted their need for more effective leadership, saying that they were "like sheep without a shepherd" (Matthew 9:36). He acted to develop new leadership patterns, modeling the need for those in leadership to compassionately serve, and be themselves people of prayer and scriptural competence.

We must pay attention to the words God spoke long ago to Jeremiah and cease the futile work of hollowing out cracked cisterns that cannot hold the life saving gospel. Instead, we need to find the spiritual passion that marks the lives of people refreshed by the living streams of God.

Leadership Lesson Number One

Good Leaders Seek to Understand Their Congregational System

Low spiritual passion is both systemic and life-threatening to a congregation. It grows within the congregational system, inter-twining itself around every aspect of church life. Good leaders learn to be skeptical of the quick fixes. Successful leaders look for patterns, and then attempt to bring about changes that involve every group and activity in the congregation.

— Evaluation Exercise —

WHAT DO YOU THINK IS
CAUSING YOUR CONDITION?

The tool on the following page is design to help church leadership come to grips with what is causing the church not to grow at the rate that it should. This exercise provides some new ways to talk about the problem.

Prepare by gathering the following statistics:

1) Average church attendance

    20 years ago_____   10 years ago_____
    5 years ago_____   Today_____

2) Over the last twenty years, what has happened to the population of the community surrounding the church?

Note that census data is often available from your denominational office or on the Internet (www.census.gov). You also may want to ask your local chamber of commerce or municipal office for relevant data on the population trends of your community.

3) Has the church's growth or decline kept pace with the community's influx or loss of people?

Multiply the average attendance twenty years ago by the percentage of population growth or decline over the same period. Subtract this answer from the number of people attending today. If the answer is zero, the church is holding steady compared to the population. A negative number indicates the number of people who fail to be a part of your congregation each Sunday due to your church's decline. If the number is positive, you are gaining in attendance relative to population.

For example: Old First had 236 people in worship 20 years ago and today has 180. The community around the church has grown by 25%.

(Today's attendance) 180

(1985 attendance) 236 x 1.25 (the population growth) 295

(Decline relative to population) 115

Spend about fifteen minutes presenting the above statistics and answering any questions for clarification. Do not allow the group to discuss why the statistics are what they are until after they do the following exercise.

— Evaluation Exercise —

DETERMINING DECLINE

Mark the item you think is the greatest contributor to the church's decline with a number "1." Mark the second with a "2" and the third with a "3" and so on. Place an "X" beside any you think do not contribute to your church's lack of growth. (Do **not** think in terms of what is true for other churches, but about your church.)

____ Low Spiritual Passion – The church lacks the energy and evangelistic zeal that attracts people to other churches in the area.

____ Leadership Burnout – The same people do all the work all the time. People are not given a chance to step aside when they have lost enthusiasm for their position. They may also feel as if they were not adequately trained for their positions or that the job fails to line up with their talents.

____ Local Context for Mission – The neighborhood around the church is changing, but the church is not receiving these people as new members.

____ Poor Structures – Facility concerns, such as the lack of parking, hard to find location, inadequate nursery and program space, keeps this church from drawing new people. The committee structure of the church blocks progress. New ideas rarely get turned into new programs.

____ Conflict – The church has had or is currently experiencing conflict in the congregation.

____ Lack of Caring Fellowship – There are not many activities for fellowship, or the activities in which people just spend time getting to know each other are poorly attended. Most people do not attend a small group or class where time is spent just asking people how they are doing.

CHAPTER TWO

Getting Your Act Together Isn't Enough

The hand of the LORD was upon me, and he brought me out by the Spirit of the LORD and set me in the middle of a valley; it was full of bones. He led me back and forth among them, and I saw a great many bones on the floor of the valley, bones that were very dry . . .

Then he said to me: "Son of man, these bones are the whole house of Israel. They say, 'Our bones are dried up and our hope is gone; we are cut off.'"

(Ezekiel 37:1-2, 11)

One day the Lord made Ezekiel do a congregational assessment. The Spirit took hold of Ezekiel and placed him in the midst of a valley of bones. I imagine him wandering around knee deep in these bones, thinking, "This is one weird dream." Bones, bones, nothing but bones. Scattered and useless, bones so dry they rustle and rattle in the wind like autumn leaves. They stretch out as far as Ezekiel can see on every side of him and they depress him. There is a deep sadness here. As strange as this experience must have been for him, the meaning of this vision was not lost on Ezekiel. These bones are the congregation that Ezekiel has been called to lead. What is more, the congregation perceives itself to be like these bones. It is not just a matter of Ezekiel looking at a statistical report and saying, "Oh yes, these figures indicate that the congregation is quite dead." The congregation knows itself to be dead and hopeless.

Think about your own situation. Has your place of worship become a dry valley? Do you hope for new programs, fresh insights, and a new moving of the Spirit, but see nothing but bones? Is your congregation already dead and headed for the bone yard, or is there still some life left? I find it interesting that God made Ezekiel walk among the bones and travel the length and the breadth of the valley. Coming to an honest assessment is important. It keeps us from false optimism.

Finding Real Hope

Bones are always "has beens;" they are never "gonna bes." Bones lack the capacity to improve themselves, and in the same sense, a congregation cannot just make a decision to be "more alive." A church cannot just pick itself up by its bootstraps or reach into its endowment funds and purchase new leadership from outside. In fact, one of the worse things a church can do is begin a new thing hoping that this thing will jump-start them into spiritual vitality. Unless a church has a culture that values personal evangelism and has a significant portion of its laity wanting to reach new people for Christ, a new program will not attract new people to Christ.

God let Ezekiel understand fully exactly how the bones felt about themselves. God let Ezekiel come to an intuitive understanding of how people's hopes and their possibilities for the future were bound up together. That is why the assessment tool at the end of this chapter is designed to help congregations understand how their hopes will influence their future. When Ezekiel is fully aware of how hopeless the valley of bones and his congregation's attitude is, God asks Ezekiel a question:

> He asked me, "Son of man, can these bones live?"
> I said, "O Sovereign LORD, you alone know" (Ezekiel 37:3).

I find Ezekiel's answer extremely optimistic. If I had seen what he saw, I would have said, "No, these bones are beyond anything even you can do, Lord." One has to wonder, if Ezekiel had answered negatively, would the vision have simply ended? Maybe this is the difference between those the Lord gifts to be prophets and the rest of us. Ezekiel had a view of his congregation that was grounded in a deep hope in the power of God. Too often, we accept our congregation's decline as a fact of life. We resign ourselves to the fact that in a generation or two this particular place of worship will be gone. God found in Ezekiel someone who was willing to travel the next step with God. When we look at our own leadership, is it marked by negativity? In searching for the people who will work with us to help lead the church toward reversing its low spiritual passion, we should not be looking for people who know the right answers, but for those who are willing to go the next step and learn.

Ezekiel could have answered, "The statistics for revival are not good." I have been in hospital waiting rooms when a family has asked a doctor if he thought their loved one would live. Physicians often will say something like, "He has a one in three chance." There is something intrinsically unsatisfying about a statistical answer, especially in matters of life and death. For the anxious family, their loved one's existence is not a number. "Can this person live?" is a sacred question. It leads us to that place where our hearts hold hope, even though our logical minds say there is none. To be used by God to bring a congregation back from decline one must first love the church, just as one loves the critically ill family member. Ezekiel stands in the midst of the bones and sees them not as any bones, but the bones of his people. They are the congregation whom he loves and serves. He will not abandon them to their fate, but instead places them in God's hands, prayerfully saying, "You alone, know."

To overcome low spiritual passion, the church needs a group of people who earnestly love it. The road ahead is one of intense prayer against the odds. A small group that gathers to pray for the church is like a spark in the midst of dry kindling. The church that has a few who love it enough to pray for it will be the church where revival breaks out. To these Ezekiels God instructs:

Then he said to me, "Prophesy to these bones and say to them, 'Dry bones, hear the word of the LORD! This is what the Sovereign LORD says to these bones: I will make breath enter you, and you will come to life. I will attach tendons to you and make flesh come upon you and cover you with skin; I will put breath in you, and you will come to life. Then you will know that I am the LORD.'" So I prophesied as I was commanded. And as I was prophesying, there was a noise, a rattling sound, and the bones came together, bone to bone. I looked, and tendons and flesh appeared on them and skin covered them, but there was no breath in them. Then he said to me, "Prophesy to the breath; prophesy, son of man, and say to it, 'This is what the Sovereign LORD says: Come from the four winds, O breath, and breathe into these slain, that they may live.'" So I prophesied as he commanded me, and breath entered them; they came to life and stood up on their feet a vast army (Ezekiel 37:4-10).

God does not instantly resurrect the bones into people. Instead, God leads Ezekiel through a series of steps. Recovery groups, in a similar fashion, make great use of progressive steps to provide a pathway for those who want to leave addiction. Steps one and two for a person going through Alcoholics Anonymous sound remarkably similar to what Ezekiel experienced as he walked among the bones:

1. We admitted we were powerless over alcohol—that our lives had become unmanageable.

2. Came to believe that a Power greater than ourselves could restore us to sanity. ["A Brief Guide to Alcoholics Anonymous" (Alcoholics Anonymous World Services Inc., New York, 1972)].

Imagine Ezekiel noticing, as he walked among the bones, each skeleton had become so dry and windblown that bones from various bodies were mixed up. Once a congregation has lost its passion for God, it becomes, in a similar sense, scattered. Various programs and activities happen without any unifying purpose or identity. It is impossible for a skeleton that has been mixed together with other skeletons to organize itself and get its life together. The first step for a congregation is to admit they are powerless over their loss of spiritual passion and this has made their church life unmanageable.

This step of coming to a sober appraisal is the prerequisite for the leap of faith that comes in the next step. As a small group of people who love the church pray together, they come to that mysterious experience of realizing that God is the sovereign Lord and capable of reviving the dry bones. This is another way to view John Wesley's Aldersgate experience when, after wandering among the bones of his own futile attempts at getting his religious life together, Wesley realized his own powerlessness. Faith came to him as a gift filling his spiritual void. He wrote in his journal:

> "I felt I did trust in Christ alone for salvation; and an assurance was given me that He had taken away my sins, even mine, and saved me from the law of sin and death" (*The Journal of John Wesley*, May 24, 1738).

What is important about these first two steps in the process is that the whole congregation doesn't need to come to this realization, but a small group, perhaps two or three, may initiate these steps. Christians today need to spend time contemplating the sovereignty of God—that is, coming to the appreciation that God's will in the matter is the only thing that matters. As the group seeks to discern the purposes of God for this congregation, they know that God has the power to save and to change this church, even this church, and to restore it to be a mighty army in service for God.

The Word of God

The third step that Ezekiel experienced as he partnered with God was a command that he speak the word of the Lord to the bones. In a

similar fashion, the next step for a congregation is reclaiming the centrality of the word of God for the daily life of the people. Many
congregations with low spiritual passion feel their church does a pretty
good job of reading the Bible. They hear the lectionary selections each
Sunday and the sermon often has some reference to the gospel lesson.
There may be a mid-week Bible study with a few people in attendance.
However, when a church has been restored to spiritual passion, there is a
palpable expectation each time the Bible is opened. The people seek
application for each scriptural principle in their daily lives. The message
opens the text and makes it understandable. A significant percentage of
the church members have daily devotional time and a weekly small group
experience where they value the personal nature of their reflection on the
Bible.

The thirty-seventh chapter of Ezekiel speaks dramatically about the
centrality of the Bible in the church today. God gives Ezekiel the one
task of speaking God's word. The primary task given to those who stand
before the congregation, whether it is behind a pulpit, in the lectern (as
a lay reader), or in the choir loft, is to clearly present the word of God
as it is contained in the scriptures. The particular message God gives
Ezekiel to speak reinforces this. God does not permit Ezekiel to say
what is on his mind; rather, God compels Ezekiel to announce, "Hear
the word of the Lord." God would do this miracle by the power of God's
word—no other action is needed.

The Lordship of Christ

As Ezekiel spoke the word of the Lord to the bones, the bones came
together. Step-by-step, they assembled themselves into human form. In
the New Testament, the Apostle Paul speaks of the Church as a body
held together and unified by its relationship with the head, who is Christ
(Romans 12:4-5, I Corinthians 10:16-17, I Corinthians 12). In con-
sulting with one church with low spiritual passion, I was startled to see
that the congregation's vision statement lacked any reference to Christ.
The statement went on for a full paragraph, speaking about how the
people of the church would do their worship, fellowship, and service to

the world with quality, love, and commitment, but it did not have one word about the primary relationship that made all of these other activities possible. Was omitting Christ from their vision statement simply an oversight by the Church Council? This omission indicates a failure of modern church culture. We have come to believe that our mission and vision can be democratically determined or carefully crafted from nice sounding words, instead of seeing it as something that God gives us. Like Ezekiel's bones, we hear the word of the Lord. However, when we word our individual congregation's mission statement, our vision is to do what Jesus birthed the church to do when he said, "go and make disciples of all nations, baptizing them in the name of the Father and of the Son and of the Holy Spirit, and teaching them to obey everything I have commanded you" (Matthew 16:19-20).

Churches passionate about their faith focus on Christ in their everyday language and practical theology. There is great truth in the expression, "nothing goes without saying," for those things which fail to crop up in our casual conversation are the very things that no longer interest us.

The exemplar congregation was remarkable for giving to missions. They sent work teams to distant places and participated vigorously in local Habitat for Humanity work. Yet, when I did a geographical study of their membership, only a half a dozen of their families lived near the church. Most members drove in from suburbs and participated because they were related to other church members or because they enjoyed the quality of one of the church's programs. In spite of this congregation's devotion to mission and often-stated social awareness, they were having difficulty cultivating new members from the urban neighborhood nearest the church, which was in real need of God's saving grace. I summarized their condition as a willingness to offer people financial help, but an inability to offer them Christ. Congregations with low spiritual passion frequently have difficulty living out their mission in their context. They may develop a vision or mission statement that captures the congregation's identity and sense of duty, but they are clueless about the unique role God might have for them on their particular street corner and at this specific juncture in history. Having a mission statement does not a missionary make; a mutually agreed-upon vision statement does not mean that a congregation will see and respond to the spiritual needs of its neighborhood.

In contrast, congregations with high spiritual passion say they are "in mission" because Christ has asked them to do what they are doing. The Master's words guide them, rather than the words on the church letterhead. Some congregations turn to the first chapter in Acts, a similar passage to the Matthew one quoted above, where Christ says, "But you will receive power when the Holy Spirit comes on you; and you will be my witnesses in Jerusalem, and in all Judea and Samaria, and to the ends of the earth" (Acts 1:8). Here, Jesus provides an ordered set of steps. First, they must witness about their experience of Christ with each other, then carry what they know of him to their immediate neighbors, then go progressively further as they spread the gospel until it reaches the very ends of the earth. Witness becomes a unified process for these congregations. The people in the pews think of witnessing with their neighbors or co-workers similar to the work that missionaries do in foreign lands. Sharing faith is sharing faith, no matter what the context.

Seeing What We Are Made Of

Ezekiel watched as God reconstructed God's people. He watched sinew and muscle attach itself to bone and the organs find their place before it all was hidden beneath the skin. Observing this rare inverse autopsy enabled Ezekiel to view the integration of cartilage and connective tissue, so that diverse organs came together to form a single unified body. Before his eyes, each bone tied with ligaments and the muscles wove into opposing pairs. No muscle, however strong, may flex on its own, and the nervous system controls the actions of each part. Even though the body is an extremely complex system, its structure does not foster independence and autonomy among its organs; the structure demands interdependence and cooperation. No matter how complicated the local church becomes as a social system, it remains a body. Its varied members are united by their relationship to Christ and his purpose for the church. The church, like any organized body, is healthy or sick to the degree its members work cooperatively to sustain the mutual life of the congregation and its mission.

When people seek to evaluate the health of their congregation, they often focus on one aspect of the church. They will speak about how attendance is either rising or falling, the state of the Sunday school, the appearance of the sanctuary, the skill of the choir, or the pastor's sermons. Each of these things is surface phenomenon. Looking beneath the skin of a congregation, one either sees an organism with a nervous system and connective tissue that works together to keep everyone aware and sensitive to the will of our Lord, or one sees a disjointed assembly of parts. If we could see what the prophet Ezekiel saw, we would ask more holistic, evaluative questions of our congregation, such as:

- Are the people of our church becoming more unified in prayer and in scriptural understanding of God's purposes?

- Is the pastor, staff, and our whole organizational structure helping us to do our mission (as defined in Matthew 28:19-20 or Acts 1:8) effectively?

- How well do we relate to the people of the neighborhood?

The Gift of the Spirit

After God assembles the bones and adds flesh, the army of people looks like it has everything together. Ezekiel pauses and notices that while everything appears to be okay, there is no breath in the body. Without breath, no life happens. The Lord speaks to Ezekiel again, and this time orders him to, "Prophesy to the breath . . . Come from the four winds, O breath, and breathe into these slain, that they may live." The Hebrew word, *ruach*, can be translated as "breath," "wind," or "spirit," and is variously translated throughout this passage. When Ezekiel is being told to "prophesy to the breath," he is also being told to call out for a spiritual change. The winds are both the mysterious forces that enter the valley from heaven, as well as the life-giving breath that enters and resuscitates these physical bodies.

This passage warns us that church renewal does not happen without the work of the Holy Spirit. Many pastors and church leaders look for quick fixes to their church's problems and fail to wrestle with the deeper challenge of leading their congregation into more passionate encounters with God. Notice what the story tells us about deceptive appearances. The bones appear to be whole and perfect once they have been gathered together, overlaid with sinews, and clothed with skin, but there is no life in them.

A congregation may work hard to improve its appearance. The church may hire a landscaper, build a new main entrance, sandblast the facade, pave the parking lot, dress the choir in new robes, and purchase a marquee. Looking good, however, can be a dead end. When we cannot see the future of our organization or remember our purpose for being, human nature launches a project. Attention to the building can distract a church's leadership from that which should be obvious—the presence or absence of spiritual life in the congregation.

Notice God does not give Ezekiel magical words to conjure the Spirit. Ezekiel invites the breath or Spirit or wind to enter the bodies and God does the rest. The miracle is outside the control of the prophet, just as any revitalization of a congregation is outside the control of the leadership. It is a gift that God alone can give. Just as the wind animates the weather of the world, and the breath animates the body, so also the Holy Spirit gives life to the church. This Spirit cannot be conjured, summoned by cheap magic tricks, or made to appear by following the latest church growth program. It is given by God's grace.

In thinking about how to assure a believer that the Holy Spirit would enter into their lives, John Wesley felt similar reluctance to say, "Here, follow these steps and you'll have it." Instead, Wesley labeled certain spiritual disciplines as "means of grace." He encouraged prayer, fasting, the daily reading of the Bible, gathering with other Christians, and frequent Communion. Inviting the Holy Spirit to return to a life-giving role in your congregation involves these "means of grace." Elevating spiritual passion involves prayer that focuses on the new reality of expecting prayer to work, scripture that emphasis the relevance for the Spirit-led life, personal witness that invites others to enjoy the new reality of God's kingdom, and worship that shines with the experience of the reality of heaven. Placing prayer as the first of these new realities further emphasizes our dependence upon God.

Before We Know What Is Happening

One does not put together a perfect religious organization and then add some spirituality. Each event in Ezekiel's vision is a manifestation of the Holy Spirit. The hand of the Spirit places Ezekiel in the valley of the bones (verse 1). He observes what he needs to know about his congregation by being led by the same Spirit. The same Spirit communicates what to prophesy to the bones and then allows the words to gather the bones and lay flesh upon them. The action of God's Spirit makes each step of the process possible. What is significant about the final step is not the sudden appearance of the Holy Spirit, for it has been the central actor throughout this drama, but the coming of life into the dead bones so that they themselves become aware of the Spirit.

The theological term for this is *prevenient grace*, literally meaning, grace before there was life. For individuals, it means that God's Spirit works in our lives long before we become aware of God and accept salvation. Our faith journey does not begin when we become aware of God; it begins long before when God places in our lives faith mentors and preparatory experiences. In the same fashion, the transition of a church from low to high spiritual passion always begins with a long period of leadership development and prayerful ground-breaking exploration into the things of God. There is a latent phase, in which the Holy Spirit is very much at work yet unseen, before the explosion takes place and the whole congregation shifts into a renewed sense of excitement over their faith.

Think of a congregation's spirituality as the true architecture of the church. The church cannot grow apart from it, nor is it free to engage in any major reform that does not consider the role of the Holy Spirit in the midst of the congregation. The beauty of the architect's full vision is rarely seen until the completion of a building, even though the

builders constantly consult the architect's plans. The work of the Holy
Spirit may be latent for decades, waiting to be revealed in God's time.

The goal of leadership in raising the spiritual passion of a congregation should not be simply to give the church an appearance of being
more spiritual. A shift will occur in the very decision making process of
the church.

- Prayer will be seen in the way leaders guide their committees
  to seek discernment in their deliberations. Stopping the
  group's activities in order to pray for needs of one of the
  members will be an every day occurrence.

- Scripture will be constantly referenced as guide for keeping
  the church on target in mission. It will become unthinkable
  to engage in any project, such as a stewardship campaign,
  without leading the people into the scriptural basis for the
  activity.

- Witness will guide the church's use of its resources. The old
  way of doing church kept the majority of funds tied up meeting the needs of the church's current membership. The new
  plan demands that money be used to reach the unchurched.

- Worship will establish the congregation's sense of community and identity. Under the old architecture, people sought
  to establish unity and cooperation by getting everyone to
  think alike. The Holy Spirit, in a spiritually passionate
  church, supports diversity and even disagreement because our
  shared worship of one Lord establishes unity.

An Army

The final image that Ezekiel has in the midst of that valley is that
of a mighty army. Most church leaders would be happy to see their congregation back on their feet! Ezekiel pictures his congregation as a
mighty army and, while the militaristic imagery may not be appropriate
today, the message is clear. God raised these bones for a reason.

The goal of congregational renewal is not to get enough people coming to fill the pews, meet the budget, and give the leadership something to brag about. Instead, renewal lines up the human energy of this complex social grouping we call the local church, so that it begins to achieve the purposes of God. I believe God calls each local church to its own unique mission. Each has its own context, its own field of service, its own personality and set of traditions that it uses to share its faith with others. In the end, people must give themselves without reservation to the good work God has for them, in order for the congregation to sustain the energy that we call spiritual passion. Like soldiers sent to hold a particular point in the line, it doesn't help morale for leaders to make comparisons between their church and another one that has a different context, size, theological tradition, or missional calling.

Measuring Up

The Ezekiel 37 story then provides a progression that lines up well with six conditions that congregations find themselves in today. If you placed your church with in the context of what Ezekiel saw, where would it be?

1	2	3	4	5	6
Dry & dead	getting a few things together	Discovering new sinew & muscle	Looking like a healthy church	Experiencing the Holy Spirit	Acting as an army aligned with the purposes of God

How do you initiate a process that will help move your congregation from whatever state it is currently in, towards the state of acting as an army aligned with the purposes of God?

1. Have you named the problem? Introduce people to the idea of "spiritual passion." Identify and define the issue.

2. Are you able to show how the church's failure to grow relates to this issue? Have you charted the church's acquisition of

new members relative to the population trends of your community? Is there widespread agreement that something must be done?

3. Have you listened to the members assess their congregation's spiritual situation? Are people surprised by the idea that spiritual passion is a quantifiable quality? Do people feel that it is possible to raise the level of passion in this church?

4. Gather a small group of people who are willing to pray about the issue. You will want to get them to agree to pray about the spiritual passion of their church each day for at least a month, or better yet, for a season such as Lent, or the period between Easter and Pentecost.

5. Get various groups in the church to do some of the exercises in this book.

6. Study together the book of Acts and note how the early church lived out its spiritual passion.

7. Ask people to pray to understand the purpose God might have for this church in the midst of its current neighborhood.

8. Get the church council to talk about the issue of spiritual passion and adopt raising the passion level of the church as their key goal for the coming year.

9. Implement the changes presented in the later chapters of this book (chapters four through seven). Seek ways to reinstall prayer, scriptural study, witness, and worship as the fundamental pillars of the congregation's spiritual architecture.

10. Evaluate your progress. Be willing to measure the things that indicate a growth in prayer, scripture use, willingness to witness, worship attendance, and other indicators of church vitality.

Personal Tasks

The whole process of raising a congregation's spiritual passion begins with you. Set apart some time to reflect upon your own level of intensity about the things of God. Do you consider yourself to be a spiritually passionate person? If you were to draw a timeline of your life, noting the attention and time you give to such things as prayer, daily Bible reading, faith sharing with others, and emotional participation in worship, how would your current level of piety relate to where you remember yourself to have been five years ago, ten years ago, and when you were new in the faith?

Does the word "burnout" characterize your current faith experience? Note how Jesus prepared for the grind of ministry by retreating for forty days of prayer in the wilderness. He always made time for prayer. Instead of multitasking and double booking his life, he established a rhythm: periods of good work were followed by Sabbath times of reflection, prayer, and limited outside contact.

As Jesus prepared to turn over to his disciples the work of building the church, he prayed these dedicated people would be in the world but not of the world (John 1:14-18). To maintain this balance, we must see our primary task as one that involves spiritual passion. We must constantly cultivate this same love for God in our own lives if we have any hope of having it permeate the culture of the church. Instead of becoming hung up on the details of program maintenance, financial budgeting, and membership care, all of which are "non-religious" concerns, we remind ourselves of the mission of the church that involves helping people know and experience the love of God.

The following tasks may help you establish healthy devotional habits in your own life:

- Set aside several hours for a personal retreat. During this time, create a timeline of your life, charting the ups and downs of your own spiritual passion. Think about how well you are doing at being in the world, but not of it.

- For a month, or a liturgical season, double the amount of time you set aside for prayer and devotional reading each day. In this prayer time, pray for the renewal of your church. Seek to discern what a more passionate spirituality would look like, first in your life, and then in the life of your church.

- Note people in your congregation who model spiritual passion. Who outside this congregation has been for you an example of faith lived without compromise? What examples from the Bible and from history are most appealing to you in your search for heroes of spiritual passion?

Leadership Lesson Two

Good Leaders Aren't Fooled by Good Looks

There is perhaps no greater formula for failure than for church leaders to busily attempt to get worship, education, fellowship, and stewardship appear to look good. These things are all aspects of the greater calling that the church has—that of making disciples of all nations. Good leaders focus on discovering the purposes God has for their congregation and seek to move the toward the church those ends.

— Evaluation Exercise —

OUR HOPES VS. GOD'S WILL

Is hope ever a bad thing? This exercise requires the participant to decide which of two hopes is the primary one in the congregation, and which is the "oh yes, we ought to hope for that, too" type of hope. Sometimes, lesser desires squeeze out the great hope of our faith. When that happens in a congregation, the result is low spiritual passion.

1. Take two large sheets of paper or chalkboards. At the top of the first, write the title "Our Hopes."

2. Take fifteen to twenty minutes to give everyone a chance to share several statements about things they hope to see happen. Quickly jot down all of these statements. These statements may be things like:

   • Hope to have our missionaries fully supported;

   • Hope to have at least a dozen youth in confirmation class this year;

   • Hope that the choir sings part of Handle's Messiah again this year for Christmas.

3. On the other sheet of paper or chalkboard, number and draw three lines. Above the lines write the title, "What _____ (name of your church) must do to be doing God's will in _____ (name of your town)."

   1)_____

   2) _____

   3) _____

Take as many answers as the group gives, possibly noting them on another sheet of paper, but force the group to consolidate its final answer to three or less lines.

4. Go back to your page of "Our Hopes" and label as many of the hopes as possible with the numbers 1, 2, or 3, which the group agrees are directly related to what they noted on the other page to be where the will of God lies for their church.

5. Invite the group to remember and name stories or passages from the Bible that support and strengthen these hopes

BONUS: PRIMARY HOPES

1. We hope that the messages are biblical and relevant to our daily lives.

   People seeking entertainment will soon find that it comes easier on the television. It is the duty of those who preach to apply the Bible to daily life in a way that those who attend in this particular place need to hear.

2. We hope to experience the healing power of God through faith.

   Churches with high spiritual passion place a high value on personal experience. Unchurched people who are looking for genuine spirituality are not interested in honoring God's invisible presence through rote ritual. They want to know God in an experiential way.

3. We hope that the music attracts people who may never have been in church before.

   Congregations with high spiritual passion want to see their neighbors come to church. They ask the people around them what kinds of music they listen to in their cars, and seek to make the church music fit that preference.

4. We hope to love God more after we worship.

   Spiritual passion is based upon heartfelt love rather than on intellectual knowledge.

5. We hope to tell people God loves them.

   Congregations with high spiritual passion realize that people need to know that God loves them. Congregations with low spiritual passion focus more upon getting people to help with supporting the budget. The two hopes directly oppose each other.

6. We hope to spend more time in prayer in the next year.

The church needs task-oriented people, but our number one task is to make the church a house of prayer. This begins in our own personal prayer lives. It may require a shift in priorities where the church does fewer activities and focuses more on prayer.

7. We hope to read the whole Bible for ourselves and discover its relevance for our lives.

Congregations with high spiritual passion get people to read the Bible.

CHAPTER THREE

Red Herrings

"The trouble with the world is not that people know too little,
but that they know so many things that ain't so."

— This comment is commonly attributed to Mark Twain, but seems
actually to be a paraphrase of Josh Billings' line, "I honestly beleave it
iz better tew know nothing than two know what ain't so" from The
Complete Works of Josh Billings, (1919).

A man once worked in a gold mine. At the end of his shift each day
he would take a wheelbarrow full of dirt up to the gate. The guards
would go crazy and sift through the dirt searching for any gold that he
might be taking home. Night after night they would examine his wheelbarrow, find nothing, and finally let the man go home. Yet as the weeks
went by, everyone in the village knew that the man was getting richer.
Finally, one of the guards pulled him aside and said, "We give up; we're
not going to prosecute you. We just need to know how you are stealing
the gold." "Gold?" the man said, "I'm stealing wheelbarrows."

Leaders often focus on who is stealing the gold rather than who is
walking out with wheelbarrows. I recently worked on this problem with
a cluster of declining urban churches. One man, discouraged by how

long we were taking to clarify the problem, said, "I know why we are dying. There are forty other churches within five miles of this one. That's just too many churches." I saw other people nodding with him. The obvious solution to their problem was to blame the competition for stealing gold out of their mine. This answer fit well with our society's acceptance of consolidation as a way to make businesses and schools more efficient. Why not blame today's problems on the visionary energy of previous Christians who built so many churches in the neighborhood's they wanted to reach for Christ? This thinking reinforced each congregation's feelings of helplessness. They were ready to accept that their church was doomed to close, and when that happened, they wanted permission to say, "We did the best we could. There just aren't enough people to keep all of these churches going."

Obvious answers often blind us to the truth. I asked if there were any growing churches in the neighborhood. The group quickly pointed to several vibrant churches nearby with packed pews. "So I take it that everyone who should go to church in this neighborhood is already going to a church?" This question drew a long silence. Then I reminded them that six out of ten of their neighbors were unchurched, in spite of the successful efforts of the competing churches in the area. They had heard this statistic before, but they still were not convinced that part of their problem lay in the diminished spiritual passion that marked each of the declining congregations in the cluster. I could see that it was going to be an uphill battle to get their eyes off of the gold and onto the possibility of wheelbarrows of spiritual energy available to them.

When congregational leaders see themselves in competition with other churches for churchgoers, they forget that one hundred percent of their neighbors need Jesus. In the case of the congregations above, they may not be able to improve their odds of getting more of the four out of ten people who already go to church, but if they can win even a few of the six out of ten currently unchurched people, they will not only turn the corner on their own decline, they will reconnect with their purpose for being a church. The guards in the story above came to think that their purpose for standing at the gate was to prevent the people from stealing the gold. They lost sight of their greater purpose, which involved protecting all of the company's assets. In the same way, church leaders today become involved with protecting their building, their membership role, and their traditions, and lose sight of the central purpose of the church—to make disciples. The narrowed focus of protecting building, numbers, and customs is inherently de-energizing. There is a tremendous energy shift that occurs when a congregation rediscovers that they have something that others need.

When church leaders spend most of their energy fiddling with the budget, comparing their church to other churches, cleaning their membership roles, building an endowment fund, or complaining about their pastor's sermons, they are chasing red herrings. The expression "red herring" comes from a practice used in training bloodhounds. The intention was to teach a bloodhound to persistently track one particular scent through the underbrush. When the dog was getting the idea, the trainer drew a smoked herring, having a brownish red color, across the scent's trail. The bloodhound in training needed to learn to not be distracted by the red herring, but instead follow only the scent he was after. Church leaders need to seriously focus on what really is wrong with their congregation.

People Need the Lord

Most of us can remember a moment when we became aware of how much people need to have a personal relationship with God. We may have tried to comfort a coworker in the loss of a loved one and realized that the person had no awareness of god's love and eternal promises. We may have watched a family member struggle without the guidance we sense faith provides in our lives. We may reflect back to a time early in our faith when the joy of just being a Christian was something we felt compelled to share. Why does this feeling become less urgent the longer we work in the church?

Low spiritual passion is a cultural condition. We lower our own enthusiasm for sharing God with the unchurched to make it fit in with the attitude we see in the other church people around us. Do people need the Lord? This simple question creates a dividing line between committed Christians and the secular culture outside the church. The American culture affirms the right that every person has to choose the religion and the amount of religious practice they want in their life. The culture at large, however, no longer feels people "need" any spiritual experience at all, let alone the one that the church proclaims.

I often challenge church leaders to tell me their mission statement from memory. It is an unfair request, because many churches have very effective mission and vision statements that are a full paragraph long. "Never mind the actual words," I say, "just tell me your purpose for being. What do you want to do? What floats your boat? What energizes and drives your church?" In churches with low spiritual passion, the motivation for ministry is vague. The mission is to somehow do something for everyone. It affirms what people want, things like fellowship, education, and quality in worship. It does not say that people need the Lord. In the high passion church, even the teenager in confirmation class can tell you why church is important. People know that what the church does relates to real needs in the world.

Can you stand on one foot and tell me what drives the activity of your congregation? This desire to meet the need that people have for God can be expressed in a variety of ways. The mission statement of the Willow Creek congregation expresses this sentiment in its own "seeker orientated," contemporary style:

> "To take irreligious people and form them into fully committed followers of Jesus Christ" (Willow Creek Church, North Barrington, Illinois.).

Notice how brief and memorable this is. Other churches have done an equally good job in crafting vision and mission statements that reflect their realization that people need the Lord and it is the church's job to bring an awareness of Christ and his healing love into their particular context. My purpose now, however, is not to advocate that church leadership spend valuable time rewriting their mission statement. I wish to raise the issue of how the culture is currently undercutting the very source from which any church obtains its energy to go on. If we cannot say why we exist, then it should not surprise us that it is difficult to get new people to support us, or to get those who are members to give with any consistency, let alone sacrificially.

Every congregation needs to convince its people that the majority of their neighbors should be going to church, or at least some religious institution, even if it is not their church. We live in a period of history where trust in institutions has declined. This means that people, and particularly those of the post-modern or "buster" generation" (born 1964 through 1981), are not looking to join any organization, let alone the church. What we need to understand about this trend is that people still are willing to come to a place that meets their needs. While people are not looking to join a church, they still respond positively to spiritual experiences. Part of the box office success of the movie "The Passion of the Christ," and of the popularity of the late Pope John Paul II among non-Catholics, was the latent need of non-churched people for spiritual things. People are looking to become a part of a community. There is in all of us a deep hunger for a place where people know us by name and accept us with all of our faults. The congregation that offers their neighbors a genuine spiritual experience in both worship and in small group ministries, as well as a loving, accepting community, will effectively buck the cultural trend against church membership and attract a growing number of people who have not been attending any church.

Low spiritual passion dulls our appreciation of what our congregation already has to offer to our neighbor. The greatest salesperson for any product, whether it is life insurance, vitamins, or cleaning products, is the person who passionately believes that everybody needs the product he or she sells. Growing churches have a knack for getting everybody involved in sales. People head home from worship convinced that they have just experienced something they want to share with their friends. In contrast, churches with low spiritual passion spiral down into a state where neither the leadership nor the people in the pew see much reason for asking others to join them in worship. They may be short changing a really great church with this attitude, even though they are faithful contributors. These leaders may have many reasons why they personally like this church and enjoy participating week after week, but they have lost any awareness that others might come to benefit from a relationship with their congregation. In fact, leaders of churches with low spiritual passion develop a knack for inverse sales. They speak freely about how much less their church has to offer than the vital, growing church down the street. They learned to see the hole instead of the donut.

I led a two-day planning retreat with a mid-sized congregation's church council. They easily posted on the board a long list of what they believed were the church's strengths. The church had a great location near the town's busiest intersection and a lovely church building. They had a well-respected and competent pastor as well as gifted and dedicated lay people who made sure the church's programs were always top notch. The second day of the retreat bogged down into an extended discussion of what was wrong with their worship and how different aspects of what they were doing wouldn't appeal to outsiders. This line of conversation sucked the energy out the room and yet, everybody wanted to weigh in on this topic. I finally shifted the topic to what they could do to invite new people to come. Soon someone asked, "Shouldn't we change our worship service first, before we try to get more people to come?" I responded, "You don't know yet what you need to change. If you asked one of your members who had just invited a new person to church, they would be able to tell you some real data. In fact, if each one of you on the church council went out and invited one new person to come to church with you this month, then you would know firsthand what they liked and didn't like."

As the planning retreat went on, several people commented upon the tendency for analysis paralysis in the church council. These church leaders recognized their own tendency for discussing issues to death. As one person said, "We are good at processing things, we aren't much good at changing them." One of the signs that a church has low spiritual passion is when leaders spend endless hours making plans and setting goals, but the same things happen year after year. Part of this phenomenon raises the fact that without passion, the people of an organization will become averse to taking risks. Only when people care deeply about something, such as God's purposes for the church, will they leave the comfortable activity of debate and take on the greater risk of actually changing things.

The church, like any social grouping, gets into these spirals of over-analyzing and micro-managing when leaders avoid discussing the main issue. The leaders at this particular retreat wanted to have a long conversation about how the pastors could tweak sermons for more general audience appeal, but I wanted them to face the more serious question of why they were not inviting others to come to their church. I sensed in this church a fear that people would reject them if they seriously invited the people of the neighborhood to worship. Church leaders today are often so aware of how the culture has shifted away from supporting organized religion that they are afraid to cross the street and ask the people that they see every day if they would like to join them for worship. We all need to face the fact that in inviting people to our church, we will indeed sometimes face rejection. There are, however, things about how others perceive us and about what needs to be changed that we cannot learn unless we take the risk. We must steel our nerve to ask and take note of how others receive or reject each invitation. In this way, we will be "disciples," a word that at its root implies being an active learner.

When Jesus first sent his disciples out to try their hand at being his witnesses, he chose a mixed group of villages, knowing that in some places the disciples would have easy going, and in some places they would face rejection. He prepares them for both experiences with these words:

> "Go! I am sending you out like lambs among wolves . . .
> When you enter a house, first say, 'Peace to this house.'
> If a man of peace is there, your peace will rest on him;
> if not, it will return to you. When you enter a town and
> are welcomed, eat what is set before you. Heal the sick
> who are there and tell them, 'The kingdom of God is
> near you.' But when you enter a town and are not wel-
> comed, go into its streets and say, 'Even the dust of your

town that sticks to our feet we wipe off against you. Yet
be sure of this: The kingdom of God is near'" (Luke
10:3, 5-6, 8-11).

Both acceptance and rejection are learning experiences for the disciples. Jesus commands them to stay with those who accept the gospel
long enough to build a genuine relationship. These will be the people
who the disciples will return to after the resurrection, and because they
have taken the time to establish friendship, they may use these homes to
establish the first churches. Jesus also tells the disciples not to work
overly hard in the places where they find rejection. Instead of analyzing
what went wrong, they dust themselves off and look for the next person
to witness to. Soon, by making many attempts, they gain a practical
understanding as to what works and what doesn't.

Evangelism in today's church should follow the same pattern.
Instead of hiding under a bushel, fearing rejection, or bemoaning the
perceived unpopularity of our particular faith tradition, we should be
encouraging experimentation in witnessing. Ecclesiastes gives us this
advice:

> Whoever watches the wind will not plant; whoever
> looks at the clouds will not reap.

> Sow your seed in the morning, and at evening let not
> your hands be idle, for you do not know which will suc-
> ceed, whether this or that, or whether both will do
> equally well (Ecclesiastes 11:4,6).

Low spiritual passion lowers the self-esteem of a congregation
to the point where they no longer believe that others would want to
join them. An even greater evil befalls the congregation with low
spiritual passion; they forget that people need the Lord.

Both Gospel and Community

People need both the gospel (the good news of a personal relationship with God through Jesus Christ) and a community of faith. Christians cannot witness to Jesus Christ without also witnessing to the church as a place to live out a life of faith. Neither can the church seek to build its own membership without intentionally witnessing to the faith in Christ that is the basis of their community. When Jesus calls the church to go make disciples, he is not inviting them simply to engage in some mass-media broadcasting effort. Nor is he allowing them to forsake the world and huddle just with each other for support. A disciple is both a person who has a saving knowledge of Jesus Christ, as well as a person who becomes a participant in a learning community. People outside the church not only need to know Jesus and his saving grace, they also need a place to live out this new life.

One red herring that sidetracks churches is overly investing in a traditional form of evangelism, such as sponsoring revival events, distributing gospel tracts, and promoting certain kinds of religious mass media. By doing this, they present the content of the gospel, but not themselves as a community for people to join and live out their faith. Unchurched people tune out the witness of these churches, sensing that the church wants to save their souls but not build a relationship with them as individuals. This kind of witnessing makes people think of the old gun slingers, who added notches to their belts every time they have shot someone. Churches that mistake this attitude for spiritual passion tend to gain new members only by transfer from other like-minded communities. In contrast, Jesus calls us to make disciples, which I believe means taking people where we find them and inviting them to walk with us and receive the gospel they are ready for it.

I heard one pastor give a very low key altar call. He simply said, "I hope we have given you another piece of the puzzle today. If you feel that you have enough of the picture to commit your life to Christ, then please come forward. If not, come back next week and we'll try to give you another piece."

Many, many more churches today pursue the opposite red herring of offering only their fellowship and not offering Christ. One church in my town has a large sign that reads, "Little church with a big heart." I suspect many people read the sign and say, "Yes that's clever, but why should I come?" Finding community interests people. They want a place were others know them by their first name and accept them. When people gather and form community, they always begin with some shared common interest. An oyster does not form a pearl unless some bit of sand falls into its shell. There has to be something to cause people to gather and form a new entity. The unchurched may be savvy enough, or at least burned often enough, to desire a bit of truth in advertising. If the grain of sand upon which your congregation has formed its wonderful community is the beautiful building, or the great pipe organ, or the handsome young minister, then the seeker who stops by will soon discover the shallow truth. This is why elevating spiritual passion is so important. When we are passionate about God, we do not forget to say that besides loving each other, we also love Jesus. We offer to the world Christ and his church. As Paul puts it, "I am not ashamed of the gospel, because it is the power of God for the salvation of everyone who believes . . ." (Romans 1:16).

We Can't Be Passionate, We're _____!

People claim two truths concerning their own denomination, no matter what it is, as opposed to all other denominations. The first is they like to eat. Every long-time member believes that his or her church has more meals and better potlucks than any other church. In fact, one of the churches I served wouldn't let me move on to another assignment until I assured them that I had indeed gained more weight while I was among them than I had in previous churches. The other truth people claim about their own denomination is that they are tradition bound, and therefore are more devoid of the passion that some people are looking for in a church. Some claim their denominational theology just isn't as "emotional" as other churches. Many United Methodists believe their doctrines are so middle-of-the-road that no one can get excited about them. Presbyterians counter that they have a whole church polity governed by elders, so they can't do anything unless it pleases them. Lutherans and Episcopalians will say their liturgy and practices go back almost 500 years, and so of course they don't have the spontaneity and vigor of some more modern churches.

Yet every church, no matter the denomination, needs spiritual passion. Garrison Keillor built his comic career on depictions of the stoic, unemotional, Norwegian bachelor farmers of a fictional northern Minnesota town and the equally passionless religion practiced by the Lutherans in their Lake Wobegon church. His characters are funny because Keillor mixes exaggerated stereotypes with circumstances where basic human nature warrants an outward display of emotion. Some United Methodist congregations have so misunderstood the Wesleyan emphasis on finding the middle way and participating in ecumenical conversation that they no longer hear the driving passion that caused John Wesley to proclaim: "The world is my parish." Some Presbyterian, Baptist, and United Church of Christ churches have become so congregational that they have abandoned the needs of those outside their congregations. Some Lutheran and Episcopal churches may have become so focused on liturgy and tradition that they no longer feel the emotional content their weekly ritual contains.

At the heart of each of our different denominations is the story of Christ's death and resurrection, a narrative so fraught with emotion that we call it the passion story. Each church, no matter what its theology, traces its birth back to Pentecost, when each believer received the Holy Spirit. It is unreasonable to expect God's Spirit to be only evident in some churches or to only manifest itself outside of the mainstream of congregational life. Elevating a congregation's spiritual passion does not require any particular form of emotional display. Instead, each congregation must work out what form of passionate spirituality is suitable for its context and theological tradition.

If Only We Had a New Pastor

Once I replaced my car's tires without changing the alignment. This was a costly mistake, as the misaligned vehicle soon ruined the new tires.

One commonly held misconception in declining churches is the belief that getting rid of the current pastor will fix the problem. Whether or not your church experiences a pastoral change in the near future, changing the clergy leadership without changing the congregational system is a lot like changing the tires on a vehicle that needs a whole new alignment. Jesus illustrated the same point by describing the disastrous results of putting new wine in old wineskins (Luke 5:37). This has led many church theorists to adopt a triage mindset where judicatory leaders send the new pastors to serve declining churches, instead of beginning new churches and improving those situations that can be rapidly turned. Unlike wineskins, we can realign cars and human organizations. I am adamant about the importance of clergy and laity partnering together to do the difficult work of systemic change in local congregations. Simply changing the pastor (either by getting a new one or retraining the one currently in office) is unlikely to elevate spiritual passion for the long term. This is by far one of the most common "red herrings" in church life today. An effective realignment of the congregation's culture will outlast the tenure of several pastors.

Not only does the current competition for effective pastors put declining congregations at a disadvantage, but the very nature of the clergy person's role limits the congregation's capacity to act unilaterally for change. Further, I am convinced that it doesn't matter whether one's denomination has an appointment system or a system which allows the congregation to dismiss and call (or choose) its next clergy, the leaders who already have the skills to reverse decline rarely end up moving to declining churches. (For further insights into how a free market prevents effective clergy from going to struggling churches, see George Barna's *Turn Around Churches* (Regal Books, 1993) pp. 43-53.)

To understand why this is, one only needs to reflect upon the three types of clergy who are likely to accept a call or an appointment to serve a congregation that is declining because of low spiritual passion.

THE INCOMPETENT CLERGY

Every year, thousands of pastors change churches as a means of escape. They fail to reverse the decline that they experienced in their previous post and search for a church that is, in some way, "better." This may be an honest case of having had a "poor fit" in their previous situation, and they may indeed find your church (or you, the pastor, may find your new situation) more open to their/your efforts at raising the level of spiritual passion.

When pastors emerge from a situation where their gifts have not been appreciated, they bring the emotional wounds associated with having fought an uphill battle. They may hesitate to make leadership changes or fear offending those who have become comfortable in a low commitment rut. They may see their family struggle to fit in and adapt to the new neighborhood and school system. At both home and work, the pastor may feel responsible for the trauma of the move and the implication of failure that precipitated it. In short, pastors often arrive at new situations burned out. The excitement and challenge of entering into the new relationship may keep both the pastor and the pastoral search committee (or Pastor/Parish Relations Committee) from recognizing the signs of this emotional fatigue.

Fortunately, churches can implement the initial steps in raising spiritual passion, which involve strengthening the congregation's dependence upon prayer and Bible study, and affirm the new pastor's needs for orientation, personal healing, and re-tooling of pastoral skills.

Pastors sometimes accept a call, or receive an appointment to a declining situation, with a stated hope, or more often, a whispered prayer, that it be less demanding than the church they have left. In their excellent book, *Quiet Conversations: Concrete Help for Weary Ministry Leaders* (Mission Growth Publishing, 2000), Alan and Cheryl Klaas argue that churches demand more than they should from staff and pastoral leaders because many of these churches lack a passion for fulfilling the great commission (one of the marks of spiritual passion, see chapter five). Churches turned inward, with no energy for trying new things, present as "easy churches to pastor," when, in fact, the lack of spiritually productive activity creates a vacuum that draws petty issues, demanding personalities, and internal conflicts to the center of the congregation's collective attention. Jesus very aptly tells the following parable to warn about the propensity that religious organizations have to tidy up their outward appearance (especially when they are searching for or preparing to receive a new pastor), but neglect the need to fill their hearts with God's spiritual reality.

> "When an evil spirit comes out of a man, it goes through arid places seeking rest and does not find it. Then it says, 'I will return to the house I left.' When it arrives, it finds the house unoccupied, swept clean and put in order. Then it goes and takes with it seven other spirits more wicked than itself, and they go in and live there. And the final condition of that man is worse than the first. That is how it will be with this wicked generation" (Matthew 12:43-45).

Jesus found that the evil spirits of legalism, traditionalism, racial hatred, and class snobbery were abounding in his generation because an honest faith no longer filled the religious community. The Sadducees and Pharisees had lost touch with the spiritual passion of God's evangelistic vision and compassion for all people. They read their scriptures, but failed to grasp the relevance of God's word for their lives. They prayed their prayers, but made the act a shallow babble of trite phrases (Matthew 6:5-7). Today, when passion for the presence of God no longer fills a church, members add to this list the additional demons of obsession about financial details, concerns about the proper use of the building, and petty struggles over who's in charge of what. Even a few of these seven demons (legalism, traditionalism, racism, snobbery, greed, materialism, and pride) are more than enough to keep pastors so busy that they will neglect their own spiritual condition and soon be as passionless about their God as their parishioners.

Stepping Stone Clergy
Some gifted and successful pastors take on the challenge of a declining congregation for a season, with the idea that their next position will

be higher on the ladder. This stepping stone mentality leads pastors to pad their statistical reports and zealously make cosmetic changes in the church for the sake of window dressings. To offer a lasting contribution to the spiritual vitality of a congregation, a pastor must value its lay leadership, love its people, and have a deep sense of the church's significance to the purposes of God in that location. This touches upon one of the special aspects of successful pastoral leadership: Good pastors balance a sincere love for the individuals of their parish with sense of call to achieve the things they feel are significant for the kingdom of God. This heart to achieve excellence in both their interpersonal relationships, as well as in their church growth goals, marks the leader whose impact will outlast his or her tenure. The desire to be "in it for the long haul" is a prerequisite for a pastor to truly lift his or her congregation out of the rut of low spiritual passion.

Jim Collins' book, *Built to Last: Successful habits of Visionary Companies* (Harper Business, 1994) speaks about how successful business leaders are "clock builders" as opposed to "time keepers." Instead of merely trying to manage a situation, they set out to build a new reality. This new reality requires steady and selfless work. Flashy, manipulative, and creative individuals may achieve short-term success, and detail oriented, skillful managers may coach the maximum revenue out of a lackluster situation, but neither brings about the systemic change that leaves an organization better than what it was before they came. In looking for examples of successful leaders in the business world, it is easy to get sidetracked by flashy cultural icons such as Lee Iacocca or Donald Trump. Collins points out that the great enduring companies of the twentieth century were led by a different kind of leader. These leaders were humble, persistent, and true to their values in the face of conflict. Rather than seeking immediate, dramatic results, they burrowed in and set about the meticulous work of developing a healthy organization. Turning from the business world to our current church scene, those senior pastors who now lead America's most successful mega churches are, almost without exception, humble, low key leaders who, over the course of decades, have blended an emphasis upon the importance of building relationships

with their own drive to make the church grow. When one looks at Bill
Hybels (Willow Creek), Cecil Williams (Glide Memorial), or John Ed
Matheson (Frazer Memorial), one sees neither a detail oriented manager
nor a shameless self-promoter. Instead, one notes their sincere, personal,
spiritual passion, as well as their commitment to spend their entire career
in one place. In his memoirs, Robert Schuller writes of asking his sem-
inary teacher how long a pastor should plan to stay in one church before
moving on. Dr. Lindquist answered that a minister should never go to a
church without planning to spend his or her whole life there (*My Journey:
From an Iowa Farm to a Cathedral of Dreams*, by Robert H. Schuller, Harper
San Francisco, 2001).

Sometimes people attribute their congregation's decline to having
a pastor stay too long. "Folks stopped coming because Rev. Dulles'
sermons were the same thing every week." Spiritual vitality in any
church leader depends upon an ever growing and developing spiritual
life. A pastor who never develops the spiritual depth to stay in one
place for more than a few years will not have much to offer in the first
place. Church leaders, clergy or lay, who work to build a better organization discover ways to keep fresh and connected to the task. They
structure their lives to prevent burnout, as Steven Covey puts it, to
"sharpen the saw" (*The 7 Habits of Highly Effective People* by Stephen R.
Covey, Free Press, 1990). If the church is an interdependent system, it
makes no more sense to require clergy to move every so many years
than it does to make the key lay people of a church change their membership from place to place. In my own denomination, I am deeply
committed to changing our church clergy placement system. I think
the "normal" pastorate should be long-term, with a high degree of
buy-in between the pastor and the neighborhood that he or she serves.
When these long ministries come to an end, the conference should
appoint a trained interim pastor to act as a transitional specialist,
preparing the church system to accept new leadership. Transitional
specialists and outside consultants, working in a one or two year
interim, have a great deal of freedom to point out to the church leadership the red herrings they may be pursuing that dampen the
congregation's spiritual passion.

THE GREENHORN CLERGY

Pastors new to the ministry may be refreshingly optimistic, childlike, and naive about both the dryness of the congregation's spiritual bones and the things that might work to turn things around. The pastor who arrives without preconceived notions of what needs to be done has a great advantage over the previous two types of clergy. Experienced clergy tend to be creatures of habit. They fall back on the well-worn solutions that served in previous occasions, without asking if the current context is different. Just because the pastor enjoyed doing a program elsewhere, doesn't mean that it will be effective here. There is an advantage to entering a new situation confessing ones ignorance, both publicly as well as in ones own prayers. One of the most profound promises of the Bible is found in James:

> If any of you lacks wisdom, he should ask God, who
> gives generously to all without finding fault, and it will
> be given to him (James 1:5).

The pastor that admits that he or she does not know how to reverse the church's decline or what must be done to raise the level of spiritual passion invites group ownership of the problem. Instead of the new pastor dispensing advice that people can either take or leave, everybody partners together to discover the truth the congregation needs. The *L3 Leadership Incubator* (Discipleship Resources, 2005) provides a structure for a group of six to twelve concerned individuals to covenant together for a sustained period of spiritual formation and group learning, one outcome of which is a Ministry Action Plan for the congregation. This plan addresses the problem of low spiritual passion. This is very different than forming a committee. The quickest way to sidetrack church leaders who want to do something about anything is to form a committee. The *L3 Incubator* process invites people into an experience that deepens their faith and hones their leadership skills.

One advantage a new pastor has is the way he or she can raise questions and offer new language for the church's condition. In this way, new pastors may serve as the catalyst to get people speaking about the issue of low spiritual passion. Established pastors must take this step much more carefully and intentionally.

Solutions to systemic problems, such as low spiritual passion, rarely emerge from having the perfect outside leader bring the answer to the church. Even Jesus told the people, "The kingdom of God is within you (Luke 17:21)." If you are a layperson reading this book, please abandon the notion that changing the pastor will lift your church from its rut. If you are a clergyperson serving a declining church, please examine the way you view your current relationship with this particular congregation. Are you hoping to escape? Do you think of this church as a steppingstone on the way to something greater? Are you willing to step back from telling people what they need to do and invite your lay leadership into the shared process of group learning? Are you willing to retool and develop new leadership skills and spiritual disciplines, so that this congregation can grow along with you? If you are a denominational leader reading this book, are you willing to tell pastors that the career ladder no longer exists and that if they wish to pastor a larger church they must develop their current church? Are you willing to take the heat as you tell committees that a new pastor will not improve their situation, but that they must do the more difficult work of systemic change with the help of their current leader?

Cause or Effect?

One could easily get the impression that the difference between the congregation lacking spiritual passion and the one that has it is a matter of optimism. The congregation that looks at the world with rose colored glasses, the one that has more hope about its future, might even score higher on the various evaluative exercises I have included in this book. Further, one could make the case that having a declining congregation leads to a state of low spiritual passion, because people get burned out and disillusioned. What if low spiritual passion is an effect caused by other factors, such as loss of hope, leadership burnout, declining membership, or bad luck? One could even argue that spiritual passion is the ultimate red herring!

Imagine that one day you encounter your old friend, Joe Hubbard. You notice that he is looking rather down, so you ask him what is the matter. He says, "Well, for starters, I don't seem to have much optimism for the future." You nod sympathetically, while he continues; "The other day I looked in the cupboard and it was bare, so I had to send my dog up to my mothers to live. She's getting kind of old and I know the dog is just going to tire her out. And to top it all off, do you know what? I don't have any money in my checking account, so my checks keep bouncing!" Would you suppose that his lack of optimism caused his cupboard to be bare, his dog to leave, mother to be tired, and his checks to bounce?

When trying to establish how things relate in life, we tend to look to those things that have a greater power to influence as causes. We also know human nature allows self-pity to keep our focus on the symptoms that we cannot change rather than taking an honest look at the root causes that will require work to fix. It is possible that a congregation's lack of optimism causes some of their members to leave, but it is more likely that declining membership causes people to question whether or not a church will be around in the future. Members may indeed drop out if they become disillusioned or burned out from doing too many thankless jobs in the church. But these sound more like the effects of something else, rather than the cause of the church's decline. Each of these items implies a deeper cause that is not a random event, but rather something that can be changed through realignment of the church's system.

We would probably tell our friend Joe Hubbard that he should focus on why his bank account no longer had funds. I believe that spiritual passion and the saving gospel of Jesus Christ are the only real currency that a congregation can have in its account. Whether a particular congregation prospers or declines depends on how faithful its people are to their core message (the saving gospel of Jesus Christ), and how well the congregational system works to maintain spiritual passion and instill it in its members. These two essential items interrelate and reinforce each other, kind of like the income side and the expense side of Joe's checking account. If he desires to restock his cupboard and bring home his dog, he will have to both put money in his account, as well as stop writing checks that he can't cover. The congregation seeking to reverse decline will need to both make sure that it is theologically rooted in the gospel (the income side), as well as support the actions of its leaders to influence the level of spiritual passion in the congregation (the expense side).

Passion is the pen God uses to write the gospel on our hearts. When Jesus lifts up the bread and breaks it, and then lifts up the cup and calls it his own blood, he knows that his disciples will indeed remember him in this act. They will remember, not because they took copious notes of the evening's events, but because the emotional impact of the next day will write it with passion upon their hearts. The church remembers Jesus, not just by repeating his words, but also by experiencing his passion.

Today, people seeking spiritual experiences often bypass the church because they find so many congregations have word and ritual but no passion. Raising spiritual passion, rather than creating optimism, reversing decline, and overcoming burnout, will be the first task of many church leaders today as they seek to attract the unchurched spiritual seeker.

What is it that today's spiritual seekers seek?

- Spirituality—Let us offer them a congregation that prays with an expectation that God is listening.

- Guidance—Let us offer them the word of God in a way that lines it up with the questions they are asking.

- Loving Relationships—Let us offer them a community that cares for their eternal salvation as well as their current loneliness.

- Transcendence—Let us offer them a worship experience that points them towards the ultimate higher power.

Leadership Lesson Three

Good Leaders Seek New Perspectives

Good church leadership involves stepping back from time to time and asking, "If I was an outsider here, what would I see?" We may assume that what we experienced week after week is normal, when in fact it is dangerously unhealthy. God often uses those whom we have not listened to in the past to provide us with new understandings about our current reality and future objectives.

CHAPTER FOUR

Prayer with Expectation

For many months carpenters and painters had been busy refurbishing the sanctuary at Old First church, and the Sunday was fast approaching when the congregation could celebrate together the completion of this labor of love. Pastor Jones had received many suggestions for what to do for "dedication Sunday." The church planned special music and a congregational dinner, and invited a number of former pastors back for the occasion. When Pastor Jones made the suggestion that they hold a prayer vigil in preparation for the special day, he was chagrined to see his proposal die for lack of a second. Since Pastor Jones was new, he didn't know that programs that involved nothing but prayer had never been well attended at Old First. The organist remembered when Pastor Smith had set up a series of Lenten noontime services with communion. The events were well advertised, yet he and the pastor had been the only ones attending most weeks. Prayer just wasn't their thing, and it would take more than a new coat of paint in the sanctuary to change that aspect of this congregation's shared culture.

Why is it that some congregations will engage in serious and sacrificial prayer and fasting without a great deal of pastoral encouragement, while others have no interest? Many congregations are content with their current habits. They have a printed prayer or two in the worship service, a few solemn words at the beginning of church business meetings, and that is as much as they need. Two congregations may be of the same denomination, size, and social context, and yet be very different, not only in terms of the number, content, and duration of their public times of prayer, but also in terms of the attitude people have about prayer. For some churches, prayer is one of many activities. For others, it is the very foundation upon which all else rests. Some churches take prayer very seriously during the worship hour, but any thoughts or expectations the people might have about those prayers actually affecting their lives vanishes as all minds turn towards the more pressing question of what's for lunch. Churches with a less than enthusiastic prayer life eventually become sidetracked from seeking relevant truth from their scripture lessons, become apathetic about their witness to the unchurched, experience lowered interest in and attendance of weekly worship service, and start the long decline towards closure. But in congregations with high spiritual passion, the prayers of the weekly worship service resonate in the daily devotional life of the congregants, who repeat them fervently in dozens of small group gatherings.

WHEN PRAYER IS NOT FOUNDATIONAL IN A CHURCH

- Members lack the spiritual courage to share their faith with others or invite their neighbors to attend their church.

- Bible study lacks divine guidance and becomes a game of trivial pursuit.

- Humor becomes secular and mundane, rather than joyful, playful, and aware of the absurdities of the divine-human encounter.

- Worship becomes overly structured, perfection focused, and lifeless.

- Committee discussion and decisions have little dependence upon the resources of God.

- Because God is not expected be the main actor in the church, there is little hope for the future and a reluctance to try new things.

All of the above will be present because prayer's rightful place at the foundation of congregational life has been breached.

Tasks

Jesus echoed Solomon in proclaiming that the temple was meant to be "a house of prayer" (Matthew 21:13). When people come into your sanctuary for worship, are they aware they are entering a place that exists primarily for the purposes of prayer? As the congregation thinks about its role in the community, do they see their most important service as providing intercession before God on behalf of their neighbors? What follows is an ordered list of tasks that move the church towards making prayer its prime directive:

I. Provide resources and events that will help "the core people," that is, your committed leaders, develop a deeper prayer life. Leaders may agree to use a particular resource in their personal prayer times for a season and then spend a brief time at the beginning of meetings to share how they are incorporating the insights into their own practice. At some point, leaders should hold a retreat together that focuses on prayer. Locate the retreat a day or two away from the church to minimize interruptions. This experience will do far more to raise their understandings about spiritual passion than almost anything else in this book.

2. Examine each prayer publicly offered in your church over the course of a month. Ask, "If God answered the prayer, what would happen? What does this say about our expectations of God? Are the people offering these prayers prepared to trust God for answers?" The point is to raise the issue of expectation, not to make people afraid to pray! The church council may want to appoint a small group of investigators to do this work and then report back to both the council and the congregation as a whole. Include a youth or a new member to the church on this investigation team. They will help keep the team honest and looking at the familiar prayers of the congregation with fresh eyes.

3. Add small groups and short-term study experiences, with the practice of prayer as the primary focus. Since many of those who attend book or Bible studies are task oriented, you may need to advertise new focus. The leader of every new small group added to the church program calendar from this point on should set apart about a third of the group's time together as a time for the group to pray. Eventually, every church attendee will join a small group for the purpose of spiritual growth, particularly the practice of prayer (see step #6).

4. Introduce into worship and other gatherings of the congregation, times when people share how their prayers have been answered. If the worship service has more than one hundred people present, place microphones in the congregation where people may come up to speak. The first week you may need to seed the group with a few people prepared to share their praise to God. The leader of this sharing time should be clear that we are looking for short words of thanksgiving about how a prayer has been answered this past week. Initially, place this segment at a different place in worship than the time when prayer concerns are offered so people realize they are being ask to think about how prayer gets answered. Branch out and encourage other groups, such as the women's group

or administrative committees of the church, to begin their meetings with a short time of each member telling how their prayers have been answered since the previous meeting.

5.   Depart from the normal way of doing worship and make each Sunday a focus on prayer. Do a seven part sermon series on the Lord's Prayer, or look at the significance of prayer in the ministry of Jesus. What is the relationship between prayer and healing in the gospels? The concept here will be to not only to change the sermons, but to change the very way each mention of prayer occurs in worship. This will be the time to experiment with adding a period of silence between announcing prayer time and actually praying the prayers. It is also the time to make temporary shifts in the order of worship in order to make the focus fall upon prayer. Are there barriers, such as musical interludes, between the mundane and the holy, between announcements and the time when people are called to be in prayer?

6.   Build the expectation that all church leaders seriously commit to personal prayer and will model this for others. Often, this means the church council must adopt a list of basic expectations for their own membership. They will say, for instance, "To be elected or continue in a leadership role, council members will be faithful members of a small group focused on prayer and spiritual growth." This will reinforce the concept that a person's fitness for service depends upon his or her willingness to model the personal activities that lead to healthy spiritual passion.

The goal is not simply to come up with ways to get people to pray more. It is to restore the sense of expectation that ought to accompany every prayer. Having an air of expectation about prayer and its related concept—that of feeling entirely dependent upon the providence of God that comes into our lives through prayer—are fundamental Christian attitudes. Churches need to restore this concept of prayer before a worshiping community can grow into the other aspects of spiritual passion. When prayer is at its rightful place in the hearts of a worshiping people, it ceases to be mere sentimental words or the rote repetition of what has been printed in the bulletin. Instead, it becomes the modern means for discerning the will of God for our individual lives, as well as for the actions we engage in as a congregation. Further, it becomes the means by which the people of God accomplish the good they have been called to do, as well as the way the church finds the resources it needs to be in mission to the world.

Raising Expectation

Notice how Jesus intentionally sought to raise the disciples' expectations about prayer. When Jesus prayed, he expected the outcome he was praying for. When this outcome was amazing, he often used the incident as a teachable moment, saying to his hearers that they, too, had similar powers in prayer. On the morning following his entry into Jerusalem, he speaks a word of rebuke to a fig tree because it is not bearing fruit. The tree immediately withers. Just as they had been when Jesus stilled the storm, the disciples were again awestruck by the power Jesus summons by just speaking a few words (Matthew 8:26-27). He did not launch into a complex magical formula, or jump up and down. He simply spoke to the tree, "May you never bear fruit again!" (Matthew 21:18-20).

Words are the substance of prayer and instruments of far greater power than we imagine. With words we make sacred promises and enter into life long covenants, such as marriage. For this reason, Jesus warns against adding extraneous words to our promises (Matthew 5:33-37). Simple words are powerful enough when making promises and when saying our prayers (Matthew 6:7). Words mark our salvation, as we confession our faith in God through Christ (Romans 10:9). With words commit great sins and hurt others through blasphemy, gossip, lies, and displays of hatred. Jesus goes so far as to say, "But I tell you that men will have to give account on the Day of Judgment for every careless word they have spoken. For by your words you will be acquitted, and by your words you will be condemned" (Matthew 12:36-37). Why is it surprising, then, that simple words will have great power when uttered in prayer?

Jesus seems to be trying to build this sense of expectation about prayer in his disciples when he caps the lesson of the fig tree by saying:

> "I tell you the truth, if you have faith and do not doubt, not only can you do what was done to the fig tree, but also you can say to this mountain, 'Go, throw yourself into the sea,' and it will be done. If you believe, you will receive whatever you ask for in prayer" (Matthew 21:21-22)

When people grasp the sacred power of the spoken word, they no longer look upon prayer as merely an expression of wishful thinking. Often, clergy say the invocation at a community meeting, such as the Lions Club, or pray at the cemetery service that concludes the Memorial Day parade. When I have been asked to do this favor, I have always been aware that the person who invited me would be most pleased if I said a few—and only a few—good words that were nothing but hollow platitudes and capable of offending no one. To pray with any kind of expectation that God might be listening and willing to act would be too shocking for the secular circumstances. But when words are spoken in prayer they are the instruments of God's activity. Prayer has the capacity to bring about physical changes and alter circumstances. The disciples must have noticed that Jesus, as a person of prayer, shifted in and out of this special use of words instantly. He modeled Paul's instruction that we should "pray without ceasing" (I Thessalonians 5:17 New Revised Standard Version).

The passages where the Bible speaks about the power of prayer over circumstances make frequent guest appearances in our worship services, but we rarely take them at face value. Unless one is in a religious community where people are passionately trying to live a spiritual life dependent upon God's answers to prayer, the temptation is to immediately bracket Jesus' words with disclaimers about how God is not always willing to give us what we ask. Noted clergyperson Phillips Brooks (1835-1893) once said, "Prayer is not the overcoming of God's reluctance, but the taking hold of God's willingness."

The Dual Dependence of Prayer

When the disciples and the early Christian community thought about this incident with the fig tree, they saw many other biblical connections, both with Old Testament prophesy, as well as with Jesus' other words concerning fig trees (Jeremiah 24:1-10, Matthew 7:16, Luke 6:43-44, Luke 13:6-9). Just as fig trees are meant to bear fruit, people of faith are meant to bear the fruit of love and God's purposes in the midst of the world. When the church fails to do its mission, then it is subject to judgment. Jesus' presence in Jerusalem speaks a note of judgment on the people of Israel for their failure to become a light to the nations (Isaiah 49:6). This points to the twofold nature of prayer in the church. Through prayer, we discover that God's expectation of us is much greater than what we currently practice as a congregation. God's plan for the church is not that it merely survive as an institution, it is for the church to become a light to the world (Matthew 5:14). This higher calling pushes us beyond our own resources and makes us dependent in prayer upon God's providence. Prayer then becomes an active force in a congregation, leading by discernment to greater understandings of God's will, and then leading us to pray again for what we will need to participate in God's will.

Cultivating an interest in discerning God's will through prayer will always lead the faithful to places where they must fervently pray for God to supply the means. I saw the fruit of this when I came to Fellowship United Methodist in Ambridge, Pennsylvania. This small, predominantly African-American congregation began with limited resources in a former funeral home. Through prayer, the Holy Spirit led the congregation first to seek ways in which they could influence the community for good, rather than seeking ways to become established as a church like other churches. The congregation soon became involved in meeting the needs of the neighborhood's poor. It became a part of the congregation's culture to accept new challenges and then depend upon God to provide the resources to meet its commitments. When I suggested that maybe they should slow down and make a budget first, so they could know whether or not the light bill would get paid, they looked at me as if I were a child, and said, "Pastor, don't you realize that God is always good!"

In 2004, they had the opportunity to purchase a large facility with a school building that enabled them to house several social service agencies, as well as their own computer learning center. Throughout this whole process, the congregation's leadership learned how to write grants and to look for outside people and other congregations to partner with them to meet their goals. When these grants and donations came in, however, Fellowship's leaders always saw them as answers to prayer. They were not afraid to get in over their heads, because their entire existence was an exercise in depending upon God to provide the resources to meet the mission that God called Fellowship to do.

From my first worship experience at Fellowship I understood that the that the people there were filled with high spiritual passion, because they allotted a significant amount of time in worship for people to stand and offer testimony about how God had answered their prayers during the previous week. They also had a habit of coming to the altar for prayer at the end of the service, as others gathered in a holy huddle to pray for the one in need. Further, they were not hesitant to extend the time spent in worship when the Spirit moved. The other aspects of spiritual passion—interest in scripture, willingness to engage in personal witness, emotional engagement in worship, and joyful hope for the future—were all present in this congregation, but the foundation for Fellowship's life was prayer.

Leadership Lesson Four

Good Leaders Model Passionate Devotion to God

Leaders need to model a healthy religious life, including daily devotional time, weekly participation in a small group, and regular attendance in worship.

CHAPTER FIVE

Scripture with Relevance

*I heard a voice as of a boy or a girl, I know not which, coming from
a neighboring house, chanting and oft repeating, "Take up and read,
take up and read."*

—St. Augustine (Confessions, book 8)

Saint Augustine describes the moment when he went from doubt to
faith in Christ. Augustine had become uncomfortable with his own lust-
driven lifestyle. Upon hearing the mysterious voice, he found a Bible and
read the first paragraph his eye fell on:

> Let us behave decently, as in the daytime, not in orgies
> and drunkenness, not in sexual immorality and
> debauchery, not in dissension and jealousy. Rather,
> clothe yourselves with the Lord Jesus Christ, and do not
> think about how to gratify the desires of the sinful
> nature (Romans 13:13-14).

Augustine continues, " . . . instantly, as the sentence ended, by a light
as it were, of serenity infused into my heart, all the darkness of doubt

vanished away." Augustine is aware as he tells of his conversion that he is not the first person to be jolted into spiritual passion by the force of scripture.

Like Augustine, Luther, and John Wesley, I too found my life changed by a chance reading of a passage from Paul's Letter to the Romans. As a teenager, the fate of all those who did not accept Christianity concerned me. I was not prepared to commit my life to Christ if it implied that the followers of other religions were condemned to hell. At a youth retreat, I was invited to read the following:

> Do not say in your heart, "Who will ascend into heaven?" . . . or "Who will descend into the deep?" . . . The word is near you; it is in your mouth and in your heart . . . That if you confess with your mouth, "Jesus is Lord," and believe in your heart that God raised him from the dead, you will be saved (Romans 10:6-9).

It was the first time I had been invited to read a passage of scripture and then meditate upon its meaning. I felt as if God had chosen this scripture as a direct answer to the questions in my heart. It changed my life. Later that weekend I was given a paperback "Good News" version of the New Testament and encouraged to read it every day. By the end of my first year in college, that Bible was dog-eared, notes scribbled in every margin, underlined from cover to cover, and the habit of daily Bible reading firmly entrenched in my life.

I present this as a way of saying that the Bible stands on its own. The Holy Spirit uses it in ways we do not expect. It is as Martin Luther says in *Table Talk*, "The Bible is alive, it speaks to me; it has feet, it runs after me; it has hands, it lays hold of me." In churches of high spiritual passion, the Bible is set loose upon the people. Both the person in the pew and the child in the classroom freely own it. There is an assumption that the Bible will form its own relevance in the lives of people, not because scholarly clergy thoroughly explain its meaning, but because the active Spirit of God mediates it.

Congregations of low spiritual passion fear letting the Bible stand on its own. They do not offer a Bible study unless a minister leads it, for fear that the untrained person might do it wrong. Liturgists read scriptures in worship without feeling or comment, as if these texts are part of an ancient and meaningless ritual that has to be just gotten through. The Bible is cloaked either in a layer of dust or in an attitude that relegates it to being a work of literature like Shakespeare or Homer. Paul speaks critically about the Jewish congregations of his day:

> Their minds were made dull, for to this day the same veil remains when the old covenant [scripture] is read. It has not been removed, because only in Christ is it taken away. Even to this day when Moses is read, a veil covers their hearts. But whenever anyone turns to the Lord, the veil is taken away (II Corinthians 3:14-16).

Notice that Paul does not say that people remove the veil when they become sufficiently educated, nor do professional clergy remove it through interpretation. Instead, Paul speaks of understanding scripture as the natural byproduct of people entering into a relationship with God through Jesus Christ. In fact, development of healthy spiritual passion in an individual's life depends upon both prayer and scripture study. The two facets of one's daily encounter with God support each other, to the point that a person will not become intense or committed in faith unless both are present. Proverbs says, "It is not good to have zeal [or passion] without knowledge, nor to be hasty and miss the way" (Proverbs 19:2).

For faith to grow deep, people must acquire a certain amount of content or knowledge. With this in mind, the tasks that follow focus on getting the Bible into people's hands so they become familiar with how it feels, how it is organized, and how its word resonates with the spirit in their hearts. People who do not hear the Bible read do not necessarily develop low spiritual passion. But when we present the Bible in a manner that assumes it is not relevant or approachable, low spiritual passion will result.

How Much Is Enough?

Perhaps no single question divides low spiritual passion churches from high ones as much as the following: "How much Bible does the average Christian need to know?" Churches that are growing assume that the Bible is important to each individual for the following reasons:

- It is the primary tool for prayerfully discerning God's will for individual lives and for the decision making life of the congregation.

- It provides God's expectations on moral issues and general lifestyle.

- Bible reading strengthens the believer's relationship with and heartfelt passion for God. Some parts of the Bible, such as the Psalms, are to be read each day as ways to offer praise to God.

- Its narrative and people are our history. When we become believers, the story of Israel becomes our story and we find our "roots" in understanding its characters.

- The Bible teaches us how to share our faith with others.

For all these reasons, high spiritual passion churches see building Bible comprehension in their members to be a limitless task. They then challenge their members to dig deeply into scripture by doing such things as assigning daily devotional readings, expecting full participation of their membership in small group Bible studies, and recognizing those who have achieve Bible related task, such as reading through the Bible in a year or leading a Bible study at a neighboring prison or nursing home.

THE TASKS

I. Set aside a half hour to forty five minutes in the next church council meeting to have each person share his or her own experience with the Bible. Ask them to:

- mention their favorite Bible verse;
- share how often they read the Bible;

- speak about any study guide or resource they found helpful in explaining the Bible;

- tell what they think the church could do to encourage Bible reading.

2. Ask a group to investigate the worship service for changes that would make the Bible more relevant to the congregation. They might want to take a field trip to another church to see how it presents the Bible. One change might be to preface each scripture read in worship with a brief comment to let the hearer know who is speaking in the passage, the context, and the relevance of this scripture. Note the condition of pew Bibles and whether or not people are being encouraged to read along.

3. Add opportunities for Bible study and start programs such as *Disciple Bible Study* with the intention of getting as large a percentage of the congregation as possible into serious study. I have found a noon "bag lunch" Bible study popular for people who may feel that their calendar is overly crowded. The three attack points—prayer, scripture study, and witness—depend up high participation in small groups for spiritual growth.

4. Celebrate a special "Bible Sunday" (traditionally celebrated during late November) as a way of encouraging personal Bible use. Distribute one of the various "Through the Bible in a Year" scripture study guides, along with a commitment card. Recognize those who completed their commitment. Have a display table where people can order Bibles for home use and as gifts.

5. Devote a series of worship messages to the Bible and its relevance. These sermons should answer some of the questions people have, such as, "What translation should I use? How can I share it with my children? What options do people with disabilities or literacy problems have? How do I know I'm getting it right? Why is Bible reading important to the average Christian?"

6. Develop standard expectations for church leaders, requiring those in significant leadership roles to participate in a weekly small group for

spiritual growth. Expect church leaders to model spiritual disciplines that include the daily reading of their Bibles.

7. Make accommodations for those who have difficulty reading. Providing audio Bibles on tape or CD is great help for those who are traveling, shut-in, or have difficulty with print. Group leaders should be sensitive to the estimated twenty percent of the population who have limited literacy. Adult literacy classes may be an important outreach of the church. Provide large print worship resources for the visually impaired.

THE ROLE OF THE PASTOR

Each person who presents scripture during worship needs to demonstrate his or her appreciation for the text's relevance. Perfunctorily reading scripture lessons without any indication of their importance conveys a subtle message. Many clergy have developed the habit of making only a remote reference to their scripture text, and then filling the rest of their sermon with their own musings, funny stories, and popular platitudes. Worse yet, some pastors go to great lengths to incorporate the latest biblical scholarship and to explain how different the ancient cultural setting is from our own, so it forces the hearer to conclude that the Bible is too remote to matter to anyone today.

If we are going to overcome low spiritual passion in our churches, then we may need to totally retrain clergy in this area. Those who preach need to approach the text with real humility, sensing that their divine calling is that of taking a lesser role and allowing the text to speak for itself. Clergy should offer explanatory comments to the degree that they are necessary, but present no scholarship that diminishes the impact of the text. I try to allow the format of the passage to shape the format of the sermon as much as possible. If the passage is a dramatic narrative, I invite the people to consider the characters and see with whom they identify. Can the listeners picture the same events in a modern context? If the passage is a set of commands, then how might the author upgrade these moral concepts to fit our current situation? Relevance needs to be the driving force behind every presentation of the scripture.

Leadership Lesson Five

Good Leaders Look for Biblical Mandates

Good leaders like to ask the "why" question. *Why do we worship for one hour a week? Why do we do stewardship in the fall of the year? Why do we visit those in the hospital?*

They keep asking the why questions until they discover the biblical mandates that establish the church's priorities and our motivation for ministry.

— Evaluation Exercise —

HOW WELL DO YOU ENCOURAGE BIBLE USE?

1. Are there enough Bibles in your worship space for people to follow the scripture lessons for themselves? Do you provide sufficient Bibles for all of your classrooms?
Yes_____ Partially____ No_____

2. Are the Bibles used in worship and are the ones provided for the children's classes a modern, culturally appropriate, and understandable translation? Does the pew Bible match the Bible read aloud in worship?
Yes_____ No_____

3. If you use an LCD projection system in worship, do you project the scripture texts as they are being read? If you do not use a projector, do you print the page number from the pew Bible beside each text?
Yes_____ No_____

4. Have you made accommodations for the visually impaired, such as large print Bibles and worship folders? Do you provide an audio Bible version to shut-ins and visually impaired members?
Yes_____ Partially____ No_____

5. Is an explanatory comment given before each scripture reading in worship, to let the hearer know who is speaking in the passage, the context, and its relevant themes?
Yes_____ Partially____ No_____

6. Does your worship folder and/or LCD projection encourage the congregation to go further with the scriptures, such as including a message outline or a list of additional scriptural references?
Yes_____ Partially____ No_____

7. Have you provided people with an opportunity to purchase inexpensive Bibles in a modern translation for home use? Do you

maintain a supply of inexpensive Bibles for "give away" use?
Yes_____ Partially____ No_____

8. In the last year, have you added a new small group Bible study? Are you actively promoting the concept that everyone should be in some type of small group for spiritual growth?
Yes_____ No_____

9. Are biblical devotions incorporated into the start of every church committee meeting?
Yes_____ Partially____ No_____

10. Have you done a "Through the Bible in a Year" (or in three years) type program? Have you recognized the people who have completed reading the entire Bible?
Yes_____ No_____

CHAPTER SIX

Witness with Joy

"I think it is because they are bringing their friends to worship. We do very little advertising because I told them from day one that they are the best advertising we have. Also because people are giving of their time, talent, and treasures in significant ways, these folks don't bicker about the small stuff like every other congregation I have seen. It is truly amazing."

—Rev. Eddie Scheler, in an interview with the author, when asked to explain the remarkable growth of Grace Lutheran Church in Bradford, Pennsylvania.

It often surprises church leaders when they rediscover the power of personal faith sharing and how that contributes to the energy level of their congregation. What is remarkable about high spiritual passion churches is not the number of people who respond to the evangelistic appeal of the messages, but rather the joy members receive from their own opportunities to share Jesus with their neighbors. Pastor Scheler mentions how his folks, " . . . don't bicker about the small stuff like every other congregation." When a congregation divides its attention between the tasks of pleasing the pastor, making the budget, having the best choir, etc., their competing claims for energy alienate and divide the church members from each other. When the congregation begins to think of themselves as a faith sharing community, they rediscover the unifying nature of the gospel. Jesus was able to keep together a diverse group of disciples. Simon the Zealot (on the radical right) broke bread with Matthew the tax collector (who had colluded with the occupying Romans) because Jesus kept them focused on bringing the message of the kingdom of God to their neighbors. Sharing with others how their own lives were changed by having a relationship with Jesus became more exciting for them than sharing the latest gossip about who did what.

Evangelism is indispensable. When the church ignores its evangelistic call, it will always fall into low spiritual passion. I found this clearly demonstrated in a very wonderful congregation, which had excellent leadership but a reluctance to engage in any form of personal evangelism. They were a young, professional, suburban, mainline church, with an excellent pastor whose doctoral thesis was in spiritual formation. The key laypeople and their pastor could articulate their faith, but they rarely expressed religion with any passion or sense of urgency. It was an intellectual matter, always shared with cautious respect for the possible opinions of others.

As I came to know this congregation, I identified a number of examples where their unwillingness to be evangelistic was lowering their spiritual passion and preventing them from living up to their potential as a congregation. They ran a successful daycare, but they never made an effort to invite the unchurched families who were a part of that program to come to church. They were reluctant to leave any Christian images on the walls of the church school rooms for fear that they would offend the daycare children of other faiths. They had some creative theatrical people who annually put on a lavish production to raise money for charity, but it did not occur to them to write a religious message into these events or to use drama as a way to share their faith. In both of these examples, the congregation gave their dedication in service to the community, but received none of the energy or new members back, which they could have received if only their congregational culture and identity was more evangelistic.

Contrast that congregation with the story of Grace Lutheran Church in Bradford, Pennsylvania. In the early 1980s, Bradford was a small city in decline. The oil refining and light manufacturing jobs were leaving town, along with most of the region's young adults. All across town, churches were feeling the crunch, as old oil wealth dried up and the membership became more elderly. Most Bradford churches had good reason to feel a loss of optimism, if not a loss of spiritual passion. But surprisingly, during the 1980s several Bradford churches did grow. These churches prospered because of their joyful enthusiasm for sharing the gospel in creative ways.

Grace Lutheran was a small traditional congregation. When a local supermarket went out of business, they bought the property so they could use the open, single-story space. They designed the worship area to house both a contemporary worship experience (a new concept at the time), as well as a liturgical ritual their older members preferred. This property had two aspects no one else seemed to think that a church needed: plenty of parking and a close proximity to the city's Section 8 housing. By cultivating a congregational culture that was highly invitational, Grace grew steadily over the next two decades until it reached 174 at three worship services at the end of the century. Recently, they have entered a phase of rapid growth, attaining an average of 289 at five worship services in 2005.

Rev. Scheler attributes this growth to the following factors:

1. Concerning prayer, Scheler said, "Prayer Life has been deepened through lay people leading congregational prayers, having a twenty-four hour prayer vigil every quarter, . . . an active prayer chain, and most of all, the public celebration of answered prayer [in worship]. We call them "PTL's" (Praise the Lord) [and respond] with clapping and rejoicing in the Lord."

2. Intentionally designed and use the building to bring people into the church. Offered programs that meet the needs of the

neighboring poor, as well as the interests of the town's general population. Recently added on a "Community Life Center," which compliments their twenty-four hours a day, seven day a week approach to facility use.

3. Expanded Bible study participation and small groups.

4. Actively trained and encouraged each member to witness for the faith. "In terms of sharing our faith, I show them, encourage them, model for them and give [them] Biblical reasons almost every week," said Scheler.

Personal faith sharing has become an integral part of the entire approach to being the church in the context of this small city. There is not one single action, such as adding contemporary worship or purchasing the old A&P building, which has enabled this congregation to grow. Instead, the whole church system has been incorporated around evangelistic principles.

Going Beyond Being a Welcoming Congregation

There are many excellent materials for making the church more inviting and improving the odds of a visitor deciding to come back. The "Igniting Ministries" program sponsored by the United Methodist Church (www.ignitingministry.org) has gathered some of the most effective resources into a handy package. However, raising the spiritual passion of a congregation requires more than just implementing a few tricks for making people feel at home with this congregation. A shift has to occur in the way the congregation thinks about faith, so they feel compelled to share the gospel even with those who may never come to join them in worship.

This begins by inviting church members to think about the difference Jesus has made in their lives and then to verbalize this insight. Small groups can offer an opportunity for Christians to reflect and share their day-to-day experiences of God's grace with each other. Set aside time in worship for lay people to give short testimonies about the impact being a Christian has had on their lives. Each Sunday in Lent, one church invites one of its members to stand in the "witness box" and give a brief account of his or her faith experience. As people become comfortable with the idea of talking about their personal experience in the safe environment of their congregation, it becomes more natural for them to speak about faith with outsiders. Gradually a culture of evangelism starts to take hold in the church.

The church can offer workshops that give people basic tools for speaking about Jesus with a non-Christian. *The Faith-Sharing Congregation: Developing a Strategy for the Congregation as Evangelist* (Shirley F. Clement and Roger K. Swanson, Discipleship Resources), and *Witness: Learning to Share Your Christian Faith* (Ronald K. Crandall, Discipleship Resources) are excellent tools for teaching personal evangelism.

Overall, even churches with a highly evangelistic culture will find that only a few of their people (some estimate only ten percent) feel comfortable actively sharing their faith. To put this another way, the Holy Spirit does not distribute the spiritual gift of evangelism as widely as we might expect. Three things need to be done about this:

1. Train, encourage, and recognize people who do enjoy sharing their faith. When a new person comes to faith through the efforts of one of these people, give the person with the gift of evangelism a role in the service when the new believer becomes a member of the church (or if it is your tradition, at the new believer's baptism service). If, however, we don't provide training in evangelism for all of our members, we will never be able to recognize who has this special gift of evangelism. The fact that some people excel at faith sharing does not mean that it isn't an important aspect of basic Christian living.

2. All people need to see that bringing someone to faith is a long process, with many people contributing a little push along the way. The person who shares a kind word and says a prayer for a neighbor may be as instrumental in that person coming to faith as the more verbal evangelistic person who tells him or her how to accept Jesus. Too often, discipleship

is seen as the task of making people into good church members. Real evangelism is the task of helping people to avail themselves of Christ's saving grace.

3. People need to realize that it is ok to invite people to attend church with them. This, too, is a form of witnessing. I often encourage people to keep with them a list of the three or four people for whom they are actively praying will come to faith. This is also known as the FRAN plan (Discipleship Resources). It encourages people to pray for a friend, relative, acquaintance, and neighbor every day, and then commit to inviting these people to church when the opportunity arises.

Tasks

Practice sharing faith with the other members of your small group. Invite each small group or committee in the church to forgo their usual business for one meeting and ask each person take three minutes to answer the following questions:

- When did you first know that God loved you?

- What event has recently made you aware of God's love?

- What has been your most significant spiritual experience?

- Have you ever tried to share your faith with another person?

Schedule, on a regular basis, classes that teach people how to share their faith. Use resources such as *The Faith-Sharing Congregation* or *Witness*.

Have church leaders talk about their faith sharing experiences with each other. Agree that for the next year, the business of the church council meeting will not begin until someone tells how he or she shared his or her faith this week.

Make frequent references to faith sharing in worship. Emphasize passages of scripture that speak about witnessing. Present a sermon series from the book of Acts, showing how committed the early church was to sharing their faith.

Leadership Lesson Six

Good Leaders Applaud Evangelism Wherever They See It

The love of God, available to us through Jesus Christ, is good news. The words evangelism and evangelical are rooted in the act of sharing this good news.

Church life is often polarized between those who consider themselves to be evangelical and those who don't. Good leaders recognize that this distinction is de-energizing. They seek to emphasize the common ground, the fact that we all believe that Jesus is good news, that prayer is life changing, and that spiritual matters are important.

CHAPTER SEVEN

Worship with Passion

The minister gave out his text and droned along monotonously through an argument that was so prosy that many a head by and by began to nod—and yet it was an argument that dealt in limitless fire and brimstone and thinned the predestined elect down to a company so small as to be hardly worth the saving.

—Mark Twain, The Adventures of Tom Sawyer

The church with low spiritual passion may have very beautiful worship led by musicians and speakers at the top of their profession, but it often fails to impress the congregation with a sense of expectation about prayer, that the scripture being read is relevant to their lives, or an understanding of the importance of their own witness to the Lordship of Christ. In short, the people participate without becoming personally involved or having their current state of spiritual devotion deepened.

Mark Twain pokes fun at the minister who delivers a message filled with awe inspiring images, "limitless fire and brimstone," and yet the sermon causes people to nod off. There is a disconnect between the emotional content of the sermon's words and the affect the message actually has upon the hearer. The failure is twofold: the preacher has fallen into a predictable routine where he no longer considers what gestures and facial expressions would best communicate his meaning, and the congregation has been trained to disregard the urgency and relevance of anything that they hear from the pulpit or sing about in the hymns. We may experience the same disconnect in our worship.

When low spiritual passion has taken over the worship service:

- Worship leaders qualify statements about spiritual truths with mushy language. One says, "Many people in our western culture find Jesus to be helpful," instead of, "Jesus Saves!"

- New ways of communicating the gospel are not sought.

- Leaders choose music they personally like, seasonally appropriate, and familiar to the congregation or within the skill range of the musicians. They rarely consider if the music reinforces the message or communicates in a challenging way.

- The people in the pew are not given any avenues for responding to the message. The bulletin may invite people to say "amen," applaud, or come forward for an altar call, but the congregational culture puts a damp cloth on any public displays of emotion.

- The language of worship is rational, not experiential. It invites us to think about what is being presented to us. It does not invite us to participate in a flow of activity that unites all present in the experience of worship.

- The order of worship is *too* orderly. Routines, ritual, and an emphasis on staying on time make everything that happens overly predictable.

The challenge of raising spiritual passion in a congregation to a new reality involves getting leaders in a worship service to think about what the appropriate emotional response is to the content they are dealing with. This means worship leaders need to function as a team.

They should meet regularly and discuss the theme of the upcoming service. Those who are in regular leadership roles need to build a relationship of trust and make changes "on the fly" that will improve the congregation's experience. They should go on a retreat together or have a weekly prayer time together. They need to practice sharing their faith experience with each other. They need to talk about what worship personally means to them. What experiences formed their expectations about worship? Each week, they need to be on the same page in regards to what they want the congregation to take away from worship and the contribution each team member is willing to make to see that it happens.

Being a member of a worship team forces the organist to think about the words of the hymn he or she is playing. If the team decides the congregation should take away a sense of the joy of heaven from the service, then what stops should the organist choose? During their years of service to a church with low spiritual passion, the musicians may have lapsed into the habit of reading the music, noting its time signature, and assuming that if they performed what was on the page technically right, they were doing their job. Each piece of music has a sensual power that needs to line up with its message. Further, the choice of music and its tone must compliment the overall theme of the worship service, as well as bring the people to the appropriate attitude for what happens next in the service.

The Problem of Manipulation

Low spiritual passion causes the church to emphasize the rational to the detriment of the emotional and kinetic aspects of faith. People come to worship not just seeking to learn spiritual things, but also wanting to know how they should feel about the things of God. Should they feel fear? Should they feel love? A great deal of influence is given to each person who leads in worship. Leaders cannot shirk or delegate this responsibility. To underplay or deadpan the emotional content of a song or scripture is just as confusing to the hearer as when a musical selection or reading with minimal content has a grand flourish. The piece of background music playing as the children come up for their message should not have the same emotional tone as the music that follows an impassioned invitation for people to receive Jesus as their savior.

Each reading also has a certain emotional content inherent in its words and works to compliment or contrast what is said or sung next. This is particularly true of the music and words heard in the first few minutes of the service. People come into to worship still carrying the concerns of their daily lives. How will what they hear help them find spiritual sanctuary in this place? What will make them aware of the importance of this Sabbath?

Our culture tends to overemphasize the power lone orators have to manipulate crowds into unreasonable behavior. Images of Hitler, Jim Jones, and David Koresh have led many clergy to adopt a casual "this is just my opinion, folks" approach to the life changing truths of our faith. If the pastor commits to using worship to lift the spiritual passion, he or she must also risk speaking more clearly about what he or she believes. Here again, working within a worship team provides the support many pastors need to be more courageous in their presentation. It also provides a check for pastors who may be using their worship leadership role to prop up their own ego.

One of the most insidious habits that pastors fall into is that of trying to force every message into the same format. Each sermon topic and scripture has its own expected emotional outcome. Preachers should cultivate this outcome and allow it to shine through at the message's conclusion. Some messages should leave listeners feeling as if they have been embraced by the tender mercy of God. Others challenge listeners to follow a rational argument and make appropriate changes to their behavior. Still others give listeners one more piece of the gospel and invite them to commit to Christian discipleship. Unfortunately, most pastors have fallen into the habit of using the same message format each time, no matter what the content. Their congregation shows up every Sunday knowing they will hear one cute story at the beginning of the message, three points that may or may not be relevant to their lives, and then a poem that marks the conclusion. At the door, people will shake the pastor's hand and say, "Nice sermon," which really means, "We like you pastor, and that was a funny story you told about the kid and his dog, but we are clueless as to how the scripture had anything to do with what you were saying."

Each scripture text suggests its own emotional tone, as well as a variety of appropriate ways to deliver that content and tone. The scripture may end with an appeal to commit oneself to the Christian faith, such as the apostle Paul's speech before Agrippa:

> Then Agrippa said to Paul, "Do you think that in such a short time you can persuade me to be a Christian?"
>
> Paul replied, "Short time or long—I pray God that not only you but all who are listening to me today may become what I am, except for these chains" (Acts 26:28-29)

This scripture encourages preachers to risk sharing from their own faith walk and saying why they, like the apostle Paul, would desire for others to become a Christian. In organizing a sermon on this text, the preacher must be careful not to let any stories or side issues distract from the message's challenging conclusion, where the hearers must decide if Christian faith will work for them also. This message, like many others, is a sales event in which the emotions must be present at the end for the deal to successfully conclude.

Resources such as Fred Craddock's *Preaching* (Abingdon Press, 1985) can help preachers fit content with format. I find that even after three decades in worship leadership, I am still trying to improve the way I read scripture. It is not simply a matter of saying the words and following the punctuation marks. Intentional eye contact, dramatic pauses, and changes in tone help convey the often familiar words with freshness. Clayton Schmit's book, *Public Reading of Scripture* (Abingdon Press, 2002), is useful here.

Not only should preachers alter the format of the sermon to fit the emotional content of the text, but they should also design the entire service to best fit the emotional flow of the day's theme. In designing a worship service that raises the spiritual passion of a congregation, routine and familiarity is the enemy. If people can predict what will happen next in worship, they will not make themselves available for the emotional impact of each segment. Huck Finn, in the passage from Mark Twain above, notices that what the minister was saying was profoundly shocking precisely because he is an outsider to this worship service. The members who experience this message in monotone each week have been lulled to sleep by repetition. They have learned once the preacher gets going, none of what follows will have any relevance to either their heads or their hearts. Simply adding better illustrations to the sermon will not help this situation. Worship leaders need to commit themselves to a greater level of integrity by linking the meaning inherent in the scripture text with the appropriate emotional vehicle, whether that be joyful music, somber reflection, or challenging rhetoric.

Building a Successful Emotional Sequence to Worship

My wife and I recently watched the movie *Alien* for about the fifth time. I was struck by how carefully the movie built emotional involvement in the viewer. I found myself wondering what it would be like for the church to order its worship to capture the attention of the congregation. The initial scenes of the movie were very quiet, almost serene. The crew of the spaceship is bored, their conversation centering on petty issues. Then, for a brief second, we see the alien attack the first crewmember. Immediately after this attack, the scene shifts back to a silent view of the planet's cold exterior. The extended period of calm surprised me. The film's director obviously realized that real suspense was not induced by constant scenes of blood and gore. For the next half hour, the director interspersed scenes of the crew's growing apprehension about a possible alien intruder with scenes of normal ship life, such as laughter, eating at a table, and the chasing of a stray cat. It was only in the last third of the film, once the audience was entirely hooked into feeling the concerns of the crew, that the movie became a dramatic, human-versus-alien contest. The director carefully scripted the whole film to bring the audience to an emotional climax in the final minutes.

He timed each appearance of the alien to ratchet up the viewer's involvement in the story. The musical score modulated to support the overall plan.

Notice that raising the emotional buy-in of participants in worship is not simply a matter of switching to contemporary music, adding a drum set, or pumping up the volume. For the average church attendee, attentiveness and emotional availability are more likely to occur if there are appropriate times of silence and reflection built into the sequence of worship. Leaders can construct a worship service that supports spiritual passion in any liturgical style or tradition. But the whole of the worship service needs to be sequenced. Just as the Hollywood director carefully considers the result each scene has upon the viewer and adjusts the length of the scenes and their position on his storyboard so the movie goers leave the theater feeling both excited and fulfilled, so the church leader must consider the length and position of each act of worship and intentionally direct it in order to allow the average church goers to depart both excited and spiritually nurtured. The goal is to position and time of each component, not so that it fits within the customary order of worship (remember, repetition and predictability are the enemies of spiritual passion), but so it helps worship be worship.

The Task

Instead of presenting a list of actions as I have in the previous chapters, I wish to advocate one change in the way leaders plan and present worship. Churches with low spiritual passion tend to have some type of worship committee whose job it is to see that all the stuff of worship, such as the candles, the choir, the organ prelude, the flowers, appear in their proper place in the standard order of worship and meet everyone's expectations. Churches with high spiritual passion tend to have worship design teams, whose members meet every week and direct the flow of worship. This helps ensure that each component has its proper emotional impact and the experience of worship is uplifting and empowering. The worship design team needs to be given a great deal of freedom. It does not exist to protect the traditional order of worship.

The team may think that a dramatic presentation in place of the choir may best serve a particular week's theme. They may choose to have one of the scripture lessons done on video, present it in the form of a rap monologue, or not include it in the service at all. The pastor is but one member of the worship design team and he or she must come to fully trust the other members. Week after week, they storyboard the worship experience, maximizing the effect each segment has upon the participants. The high spiritual passion church may still have some type of committee in charge of the stuff of worship, but the leadership that works on the weekly worship design team is in a lead position to raise the spiritual passion of the congregation.

Leadership Lesson Seven

Good Leaders Are Not Afraid of Emotion

Good church leaders understand that worship should be an emotional experience. When a church committee discussion sparks an uncomfortable level of emotion, good leaders do not run from potential conflict, but rather recognize that the issues under discussion may be vital to the church. Sometimes people need elevated emotions in order to talk about the things that are central to faith and life together.

CHAPTER EIGHT

The Money Will Be There

Elevating the church's spiritual passion means lifting its heart for missions. It means getting people interested in programs and activities that teach prayer, scripture reading, and faith sharing. It means becoming more intentional about worship, and possibly making leadership changes. Raising these expectations and adding these programs is often expensive. The real disruption to the budget comes when the Spirit of God begins to challenge people with a compelling vision for change. When people are praying and discerning God's will for their congregation, they often become aware that the church could do so much more to reach their community if only they did "_____." That blank may be filled in with a building project to provide a place for recreational programs that will reach disadvantaged youth. That blank may be filled in by the desire to start a contemporary service to reach unchurched religious seekers. That blank may be filled in by an opportunity to send work teams out of the church to do short term volunteer work in a mission field. Whatever the blank gets filled in with, it will require church leaders trust even more in God's ability to provide the resources to meet the challenge God has laid upon our hearts.

When the congregation seeks to fulfill its mission rather than simply survive, there is often a dramatic increase in the expense side of its budget. A plane consumes more fuel when it starts to fly than it does idling at the boarding gate. Churches with low spiritual passion find themselves with inadequate fuel in their tanks and a mentality of scarcity. They tend to have lackluster stewardship, evidenced by a lower number of people tithing (giving ten percent of their income to the church), as well as a tendency to depend upon fundraisers to meet routine expenses. This is not because these churches haven't done stewardship drives or provided sufficient material on the importance of tithing or the desperate state of the budget. People who are not passionate about something are not motivated to give sacrificially towards it. Passion drives giving. What a people grow to love determines how they allocate their expendable income. Jesus says:

> "Do not store up for yourselves treasures on earth, where moth and rust destroy, and where thieves break in and steal. But store up for yourselves treasures in heaven, where moth and rust do not destroy, and where thieves do not break in and steal. For where your treasure is, there your heart will be also.

> "The eye is the lamp of the body. If your eyes are good, your whole body will be full of light. But if your eyes are bad, your whole body will be full of darkness. If then the light within you is darkness, how great is that darkness!

> "No one can serve two masters. Either he will hate the one and love the other, or he will be devoted to the one and despise the other. You cannot serve both God and Money" (Matthew 6:19-24).

Jesus connects passion and money in a way that should make most of us uncomfortable. He begins by talking about heart, which is a synonym for passion. What you are passionate about is nearest to your heart. If your passion's treasure is heaven, then your heart will lead you there someday. Earlier, Jesus said that those who are pure in heart (or passion) will be blessed with the ability to see God (Matthew 5:8), implying that encountering God, both in this world and in the next, requires a particular kind of spiritual passion—one that is pure in motives, untainted by materialism, and focused on God alone.

Jesus goes on to say that just as the eyes admit light into our lives, so the gateway of our heart, or our passions, admit either light or darkness into our being. Just as the passions of our hearts can be either true and godly or selfish and evil, so the passions of a congregation can be spiritual or worldly. Remember that when we enter into a worshiping relationship with each other and form a congregation, we are forming a body (literally incorporating) and that body has a spiritual personality that is more than the sum of its parts. In every congregation there are individuals who are good, loyal, faithful, and true, as well as individuals who are self-seeking, cynical, divisive, and false. By God's grace, the congregation becomes an interactive system, often leading us to be far better people than we would be on our own. God does not call us to seek only the most perfect individuals to join our congregation, nor permit us to remove the "bad apples" from our barrel. Instead, we prayerfully seek to mold the system and fashion the format of our congregational organization around biblical principles in hopes that God will use it as an instrument to change our lives and to witness to Christ's saving presence in our world.

The spiritual passion of a congregation is the gateway that admits light and faith into all parts of its operation, dispelling the darkness of doubt. When a congregation elevates its spiritual passion, the light of renewed faith reaches into the places where darkness once ruled. Certain groups, such as the choir or the older women's circle, may be hotbeds for gossip and negativity. They will face a choice to either be transformed and relinquish their petty concerns, or retreat further into the darkness and isolate themselves from the renewal experienced by the rest of the church. Often, when spiritual passion is raised in a congregation, one begins to hear laughter in committee meetings that where previously somber affairs. Light and joy are outward symbols of the restoration of hope that occurs when a church becomes spiritually awakened. But the most obvious transformation occurs in the area of church finances and the stewardship of its members.

In the final part of the passage quoted above, Jesus speaks about how materialism and the service of God are polar opposites. Taken together with the previous verses, Jesus is saying that our passions (heart) guide our service and activities. Any idolatrous honoring of money or material things puts us in opposition to God. A congregation may state that they intend to honor God in all things, but if their action demonstrates that their real passion is this material world, then they will drift away from devotion to God. How we behave fashions how we believe, and many congregation have fallen away from high spiritual passion and the pure love of God by acquiescing to the world's love of money.

What does spiritual passion have to do with stewardship and the church's capacity to fund its budget? It has everything to do with these things. First of all, as mentioned before, a church leader's ability to convince members to set aside a significant portion of their income for God's purposes directly relates to the congregation's level of spiritual passion. To put it another way, the degree to which the congregation is in love with God determines the expectations the people will hold about giving. They will set the bar of sacrificial giving higher and higher, once they come alive to the joy of faith.

Second, and just as importantly, the high spiritual passion congregation will have far less patience for seeing their money placed into savings when it could be achieving some immediate good for the kingdom of God. One high spiritual passion church recently completed a building project and was carrying a large mortgage, when a lapsed member died without an heir and left the church sufficient money in his will to extinguish the church's debt. However, when the church council received the bequest, it did not choose to pay off the mortgage, but instead hired a youth director and gave joyfully to several local mission projects. As one council member put it, "We figured God gave us this money today for a reason and it didn't seem right just giving it all back to the bank."

For this reason, I make the following general observation; when a congregation begins to decline and lags into low spiritual passion, some-one on the finance committee will always suggest that the church develop an endowment fund so they will be able to maintain their ministries, even when there a fewer people to support them. This reasoning is part of the sickness. The opposite is also true. Whenever a congregation begins to feel more passionately about the things of God, there soon arises some avenue, which if taken, will require an all out effort to give sacrificially. This may be the challenge to do a major mission project, to start a new worship service, or to add on to their building. If the con-gregation accepts the challenge and launches a major stewardship drive for the purpose of doing this new thing, then their spiritual passion will kick up to an even higher notch. For the congregation of high spiritual passion, the more they give, the more they grow—both in numbers, as well as in love for the Lord.

Leadership Lesson Eight

Good Leaders Focus on Building Passion, Not on Containing Expenses

Leaders are responsible for looking for
possibilities and spiritual challenges.
It means more than managing expenses and
tracking cash flow. The church always needs
good managers in order to maintain high
integrity concerning our finances and to be
the best stewards of what we have received.
But managers are not meant to be leaders.
Good Leaders focus on the goals, passion,
and resources of the congregation,
not on containing expenses.

CHAPTER NINE

The Bones Become an Army

"Blessed are you when people insult you, persecute you and falsely say all kinds of evil against you because of me. Rejoice and be glad, because great is your reward in heaven, for in the same way they persecuted the prophets who were before you."

—Matthew 5:11-12

The bad news is that it is impossible to elevate the spiritual passion of a group of people without elevating the amount of conflict they perceive between themselves and the world at large. In many passages, Jesus talks about the costs of discipleship. He says how those who follow his lead and model the Christian life will stand out. Being passionate about faith does make you different. It puts one in the crosshairs of a world gunning for non-conformists. Jesus does not offer a witness protection program for those who take on the challenge of sharing their faith.

Individuals who recover their love for God become prophetic, speaking the truth they have come to know on a personal level, both in season and out (2 Timothy 4:2). Congregations led by passionate people cannot help but enter into a love-hate relationship with the popular culture that surrounds them. Churches that have high spiritual passion often impress the secular culture with their savvy use of advertising, willingness to make use of cultural icons, and their mastery of current technology. Outsiders say, "Hey, these churches are really speaking our language." But the content of what these contemporary churches are saying shocks these unchurched people when they look closer. Passionate churches, no matter where they are on the theological spectrum, find themselves speaking against the materialism, racism, and the secularizing influences of our day, similar to the prophets of old.

It may be that this fear of becoming offensive keeps many congregations in a state of low spiritual passion. It is hard to take the offense in terms of elevating the spiritual state of one's community without becoming offensive. Many church leaders will read this book, set it aside, and say, "That's nice, but it won't fly in my church." They may recognize that too few people in their congregation want to risk becoming offensive. Further, they may not have the courage to attack the congregation's current ways of doing prayer, scripture texts, faith sharing, and worship. There is no shame in remaining a declining congregation, but there is no future in it either!

The good news is that the vision God showed Ezekiel is coming to pass. We do see congregation's go from hopeless states of being nothing but dry bones to rising up as mighty armies serving the Lord's purposes. They take the offensive by prayerfully discerning the role God wishes them to play in the midst of their community. They become more excited about the things of God as they discover the relevance of the scriptures. They risk being considered "religious nuts" as they passionately share their faith with their neighbors. They empower teams to create worship experiences that thrill the emotions and communicate the healing power of God. They do all these things, and as they do, God makes them alive. As one pastor put it when speaking about the turn around of his church, "It's not anything I am doing. It's a God thing."

— Evaluation Exercise —

THE FINAL TEST

Rate where your church is today: _____ (date)

Rate where your church is after applying the concepts of this book: _____ (date, one year later)

1. People have hope for the future, and do *not* believe that the best days of this church are in the past:

Needs Much Improvement	Still Needs Work	Our Spiritual Passion Is Evident!
    0 — 1 — 2 — 3 — 4 — 5 — 6 — 7 — 8 — 9 — 10

2. People frequently share the joy of helping someone else become a Christian in worship and in our small groups:

Needs Much Improvement	Still Needs Work	Our Spiritual Passion Is Evident!
    0 — 1 — 2 — 3 — 4 — 5 — 6 — 7 — 8 — 9 — 10

3. People constantly share how God answers their prayers:

Needs Much Improvement	Still Needs Work	Our Spiritual Passion Is Evident!
    0 — 1 — 2 — 3 — 4 — 5 — 6 — 7 — 8 — 9 — 10

4. The church council sets goals that so excite people that the church is constantly changing:

Needs Much Improvement	Still Needs Work	Our Spiritual Passion Is Evident!
    0 — 1 — 2 — 3 — 4 — 5 — 6 — 7 — 8 — 9 — 10

5. Most of our regular church members attend a weekly Bible study or small group for spiritual growth, and we are intentionally starting small groups to involve everyone:

Needs Much   Still   Our Spiritual
Improvement   Needs Work   Passion Is Evident!
    0 — 1 — 2 — 3 — 4 — 5 — 6 — 7 — 8 — 9 — 10

6. People want to improve the church facility because they want to use the church as a resource for helping their neighbors know Jesus:

Needs Much   Still   Our Spiritual
Improvement   Needs Work   Passion Is Evident!
    0 — 1 — 2 — 3 — 4 — 5 — 6 — 7 — 8 — 9 — 10

7. Worship is never boring; it challenges and inspires all ages:

Needs Much   Still   Our Spiritual
Improvement   Needs Work   Passion Is Evident!
    0 — 1 — 2 — 3 — 4 — 5 — 6 — 7 — 8 — 9 — 10

8. Our congregation feels alive and the numbers reflect it. There are more people in worship, more kids in church school, and more volunteers to keep up with the new programs we keep adding:

Needs Much   Still   Our Spiritual
Improvement   Needs Work   Passion Is Evident!
    0 — 1 — 2 — 3 — 4 — 5 — 6 — 7 — 8 — 9 — 10

9. The key church leaders often engage in times of just praying, and they are the first to sign up for slots of time when we have a prayer vigil. These leaders' personal spiritual disciplines have become a model for everyone in the church:

Needs Much   Still   Our Spiritual
Improvement   Needs Work   Passion Is Evident!
    0 — 1 — 2 — 3 — 4 — 5 — 6 — 7 — 8 — 9 — 10

10. Not only are there fun times in fellowship, but everyone who visits with us senses this congregation has a deep joy in the Lord and is willing to proclaim that God is good:

Needs Much Improvement	Still Needs Work	Our Spiritual Passion Is Evident!

0 — 1 — 2 — 3 — 4 — 5 — 6 — 7 — 8 — 9 — 10

Total score _____

_____ % improved over a year ago.

Other Books by Bill Kemp

Spiritual passion is the fuel that keeps a congregation active and excited about the faith it has to share with the world. Without spiritual passion, a church, no matter its size, will either crash and burn or become a hollow shell of its former glory. Just as the body is fueled by a nutritious diet, so a church is fueled by a healthy, passionate, spirituality. There are, however, other measures of church vitality.

- The second book of this series, *Peter's Boat*, deals with all of the various causes of burnout. How do we prevent loss of our own zeal, as well as, the exhaustion of our fellow church workers, as we struggle to keep our church in the air?

- The third book of this series, *Jonah's Whale*, discusses how to keep the congregation united behind a common vision. How do we get to where we are going unless we know where it is and what path we should take towards it?

- The fourth book in the series, *Saul's Armor*, looks at facility issues, as well as the problem of creating a flexible and dynamic committee structure in your church so that programs are supported (rather than hindered) by your administrative process.

- The fifth book of this series, *David's Harp*, deals with preventing, managing, and transitioning out of conflict. Every pilot must communicate and respond to negative information in order avoid stormy weather and collisions with other planes. We tend to treat conflict as an unwelcome intruder, rather than a routine part of flying. This book helps church leaders not to panic, but to see God's purposes in stressful situations.

- The sixth book of this series, *Jesus' New Command*, deals with how to unite the congregation into a strong faith community. Love is like oxygen, vital to the maintenance of church life. This book provides tools for building intimate small groups while encouraging the congregation to be welcoming to new-comers.

Each of the six books of this series will focus on problems that can become woven into a congregation's very culture, and so need the coordinated work of many people to achieve change. The emphasis, then, will be upon cultivating a broad leadership base that is aware of the issue and implementing systemic changes. These books provide a common language that the laity and clergy can use together when they talk about the things that influence the success of their congregation.

Holy Places, Small Spaces (Discipleship Resources, 2005) looks at how small-church fellowships are faring compared to other congregations. It addresses the critical clergy supply problem and charts the changes that must take place for there to be a hopeful future of survival and growth for these congregations.

The Church Transition Workbook (Discipleship Resources, 2004) describes a step-by-step process that will enable the church to get moving again after traumatic conflict or being "run over by change." It keeps laity and clergy on the same page, as the church redefines pastoral relationships. The book includes stories, practical tools, and activities that will help the church see its current reality and the possibilities for ministry.